Nuggets

RECIPES GOOD AS GOLD

The Junior League of Colorado Springs, Inc.
Colorado Springs, Colorado

The purpose of the Junior League is exclusively educational and charitable. The organization's aims are to promote voluntarism, to develop the potential of its members for voluntary participation in community affairs and to demonstrate the effectiveness of trained volunteers.

All profits earned from the sale of **NUGGETS** will be returned to the community to support a variety of projects undertaken by the Junior League of Colorado Springs.

First Printing	March, 1983	10,000 copies
Second Prining	June, 1983	15,000 copies
Third Printing	October, 1985	10,000 copies

To order additional copies of **NUGGETS**, use the order blanks provided in the back of the book or write:

NUGGETS
Junior League of Colorado Springs
P.O. Box 1058
Colorado Springs, CO 80901

Graphic Design: Bob Rosamond, Sindt Advertising

ISBN: 0-9609930-4-5
Library of Congress Catalog Card Number: 82-083706

Printed in the United States of America
by
S.C. Toof & Co.
Memphis, Tennessee

FOREWORD FROM THE COOKBOOK COMMITTEE

Before you begin cooking with **NUGGETS**, we want you to know some things about the book which will help you have the best cooking experience ever! As with most cookbooks, **NUGGETS** has a style all its own. Listed below are a few editorial decisions which will assist you:

1. An oven temperature presumes that you have preheated the oven.

2. When we say eggs, we mean large eggs.

3. "Season to taste" means adding salt and pepper to your taste.

4. Heavy cream and whipping cream are one and the same.

5. The fat content of milk is your choice except where specified.

We have included a symbol to help you through busy days. The PICK identifies those recipes in which total preparation time is no more than 15 minutes. Freezing or chilling may be needed beyond that time, but your attention will not be required.

We have listed the ingredients according to their order of use. We suggest you use fresh ingredients in all recipes whenever possible. You will find the recipes for each chapter listed in alphabetical order on the divider page for that section. Recipes are also listed in the index in the back of the book by category, title and major ingredient.

We are proud to present this superlative collection of culinary creations. We know you will discover a gold mine of recipes in **NUGGETS**! Happy prospecting!

Bette Storms, **Chairman**
Sherry Maxwell, **Marketing Chairman**

Patti Anderson	Charlotte Kimberlin
Jean Bodman	Valerie Kruczynski
Leslie Bois	Nancy McConnell
Margie Cole	Heather Palmer
Jeralynn Dix	Barbara Roberts
Rondi DuCharme	Joan Silver
Sherry Goldston	Mary Ellis Smith
Jeri Hibbard	Susan Suggs

INTRODUCTION

When the nuggets of the world's richest gold camp began tumbling down Pikes Peak from Cripple Creek during the Gay Nineties, the residents of Colorado Springs found themselves smothered in money.

The gold changed forever the tempo of General Palmer's sedate resort. The new wealth drew from everywhere swarms of specialists in that most cheering of human arts, fine cuisine. Among them was Chester Alan Arthur, son of the 21st President of the United States. Arthur turned up at Pikes Peak in 1900 with gourmet tastes learned from living in Paris where he frequently dined with the Prince of Wales.

Spencer Penrose descended from his Cripple Creek mine to disseminate standards for dining learned from that elitist group of gourmets, Philadelphia's Rabbit Club. In 1912, Penrose and Chester Alan Arthur founded the Cooking Club, the male members of which gave their undivided attention to wrecking their wives' kitchens once a month preparing gastronomic wonders such as Filets des Pigeons à la Pompadour or Escalope de Veau, Sauce Genoise. In time the wives rebelled. Penrose met their protests by giving the Cooking Club its own kitchen and meeting quarters on the slopes of Cheyenne Mountain.

It should not be imagined that over the years the ladies of Colorado Springs were less active than the men in the pursuit of the art of fine cuisine. Through the past years the North Enders and the Broadmoor crowd vied with one another to create exquisite repasts. Feasts of epic proportions emerged from Julie Penrose's kitchen at El Pomar, from Virginia Baldwin's at the Trianon, from Ethel Carlton's in Pine Valley, and from the homes on Wood Avenue of such epicures as Alice Bemis Taylor and Phillip B. Stewart.

And now the Junior League of Colorado Springs continues the high gustatory standards of the past. Their new cookbook, **NUGGETS**, is tied to the great tradition that began with the discovery of gold at Cripple Creek. It explores with gusto today's approach to an art that has never ceased to fascinate the people of the Pikes Peak region.

Marshall and E. J. Sprague

TABLE OF CONTENTS

ACKNOWLEDGMENTS

The Cookbook Committee expresses grateful appreciation to League members and friends who contributed recipes to **NUGGETS.**

Carolyn Abraham
Harriet Abrahm
Liz Aikin
Lorraine Anderson
Patti Anderson
Frances Armstrong
Patty Armstrong
Mina Arnn
Nancy Arnn
Alice Aronovitz
Beth Austin
Kathy Austin
Jane Bach
Carol Baker
Yvonne Baker
Jan Baron
Kathleen Bates
Olive Bear
Mary Beltz
Joy Bennett
Malina Bennett
Olivia Bennett
Gail Berglund
Fran Berniger
Jean Bodman
Harriet Bois
Leslie Bois
Nancy Borden
Cheryl Bowman
Marilynn Bradish
Anne Bradley
Barbara Bradley
Ann Brosh
Caroline Brown
Charlotte Brown
Fred Brown
Joan Brumage
Irene Budd
Susan Burghart
Sally Bussey
Pam Cage
Alina Carris
Christine Carter
Ellen Casey
Kaye Caster
Elizabeth Chatfield
Judy Chilsen
Linda Clancy
Fayette Clark
Mary Ann Clark
Jacquie Cobb
Marty Cogswell
Margie Cole
Patricia Cole
Helen Cool
Sue Corcoran
Adele Cornelius
JoAnn Corrigan
Mary Corrigan
Joan Cox
Linda Craddock
Virginia Cresap
Caroline Daniels
Elizabeth Daniels
Phyllis Davis
Kay Dawson
Gwen DeGeare
Lana DeMarco
Carlene Decker
Jeralynn Dix
Anita Dobbin
Lyn Doyon
Suzanne DuBois
Rondi DuCharme
Pam Dymek
Georgia Edmondson

Mary Eiber
Kathe Eller
Sharon Enoch
Sally Fallon
Maria Faulconer
Lesley Flaks
Jean Flanigan
Susan Foerster
Dianne Foss
Chrysandra Fotenos
Kris Frank
Cheri Freeman
Kathleen Gamblin
Marcia Gardner
Nancy Gilbert
Sherry Goldston
Marlene Goodbar
Jane Gorab
Micky Gordon
Kay Gray
Linda Gregory
Marcia Hafemeister
Ann Hair
Kaye Hallam
Sherri Halstead
Sharon Hamann
Gratia Bell Haney
Jule Haney
Marcia Hanson
Barbara Harrison
Henri Hart
Lucy Harwood
Joan Hazard
Jane Hecox
Mary Heelan
Mimi Heim
Mary Henson
Leslie Herzog
Jeri Hibbard
Jo Higginbotham
Marilyn Hill
Margaret Hillman
Cindy Hirsig
Sharon Holland
Helen Hoover
Jeri Howells
Molly Hoyle
Myra Hudson
Betty Humphries
Terri Jacobs
Ellie Jeffers
Barbara Jennings
Josephine Johnson
Marilyn Johnson
Sharon Johnson
Charlene Johnston
Mary Ellen Judd
Mary Kanas
Ruth Ann Kelsey
Meg Kendall
Tweed Kezziah
Charlotte Kimberlin
Eileen Kin
Jean King
Frances Knutson
Bonnie Kollen
Patty Korf
Dorothy Kraemer
Lyn Krause
Donna Kring
Denise Krug
Peggy Kunkel
Karen Kunstle
Margot Lane
Sherry Langley
Connie Lee
Barbara Lewis

Patty Lewis
Peggy Litwhiler
Barb Lohman
Jean Long
Toni Long
Virginia Long
Camille Loo
Kathy Loo
Phyllis MacDougall
Nancy MacGregor
Wendy Mahncke
Suzy Marold
Pam Marsh
Marianne Martin
Verni Martz
Kathy Mason
Linda Matthiesen
Michael Maxwell
Sherry Maxwell
Cynthia May
Nancy May
Nini Maytag
Jan McCauley
Lyndell McEntyre
Connie McKenna
Marianne McKoane
Mary Ellen McNally
Gail Meis
Georgia Mertens
Sissie Miles
Sally Miller
Ann Milton
Barbara Moothart
Carol Morgan
Patty Muchmore
Bette Mulholland
Connie Murray
Mary Bethé Neely
Janet Neese
Esther Nichols
Margaret Nicoll
Judy Norman
Wendy Norman
Peggy Norton
Marianne O'Brien
Gretchen Ochs
Margaret Oliver
Muriel Ostien
Susan Pack
Heather Palmer
Lynn Pattee
Barbara Patterson
Helen Pazera
Rose Pazera
Marcia Peacore
Lynn Pelz
Lynn Peterson
Barbara Philips
Pat Price
Norma Lee Quinlan
Katie Ralston
Barbara Reeves
Ann Reich
Ann Reid
Lee Renfrow
Linda Renneberger
Audrey Richardson
Myrna Richardson
Barbara Roberts
Marilyn Roberts
Debbie Robinson
Barbara Ross
Lucy Ross
Marcia Roulier
Kaye Rowan
Lynnette Ryden

Linda Sabo
Linda Sanden
Jamie Sauer
Mary Schade
Mary Schmidt
Mary Jo Schroeder
Carolyn Schwartz
Shirley Scott
Frances Seelig
Bernard Sherman
Linda Short
Nettie Short
Joan Silver
Mary Ann Simpson
Zelma Simpson
Fred Sindt
Karen Skilbred
Carol Smith
Lou Smith
Marge Smith
Mary Ellis Smith
Mary Smith
Kit Spahn
Lyn Speer
Evie Stark
Lory Stevenson
Janet Stone
Bette Storms
Bill Storms
Susan Suggs
Susan Susemihl
Rosemary Syverson
Virginia Teichmann
Ruth Tepley
Sharon Tepper
Hester Thatcher
Terry Thatcher
Lucy Thiele
Caryl Thomason
Jean Thomson
Cheryl Tolley
Marge Tompkins
Carol Truax
Susan Tumblison
Dorothy Turner
Joyce Turner
Frankie Tutt
Melinda Vance
Anne Walker
Jeanie Walker
Mickey Wallace
Susan Wallnutt
Cindy Walsh
Patti Warner
Jane Warren
Jill Wasinger
Fay Watkins
Betty Watt
Renee Waymire
Barbara Webb
Ruth Weed
Nancy Weller
Mary Westermo
Brenda Whitlock
Martha Wicklund
Kay Wieder
Mary Wild
Susan H. Williams
Susan S. Williams
Mary Lou Wilmot
Ann Winslow
Jane Wisner
Mary Wood
Esther Jane Worrell
Ann Young
Dianne Young
Susan Zook

APPETIZERS AND BEVERAGES

AMERICAN INDIANS were the first to discover the
wonders of the Pikes Peak Region, including the natural
phenomenon now known as the GARDEN OF THE GODS.
The earliest tribes of Indians in the area were probably
the Utes, who were hunter-gatherers. They lived this
simple life until the Spanish introduced them to the horse.
The horse made the Utes competitors for the buffalo and
put them in conflict with other Colorado tribes such as the
Arapaho and Cheyenne. The exotic shapes and colors of
the rock formations in the Garden of the Gods led the
Indians to believe gods lived there. The unusual formations
of Kissing Camels, Balanced Rock and Steamship Rock
are as mystifying and delightful to today's viewer as
they were to the first Indians.

APPETIZERS AND BEVERAGES

SCRUMPTIOUS SHRIMP DIP
YIELD: 3 cups
"Everybody loves it!"

1 8-ounce package cream
cheese, softened
½ cup butter, softened
1 4¼-ounce can de-veined
medium shrimp
8 ounces fresh shrimp; cooked,
peeled, de-veined and cut into
bite-size pieces

1 4-ounce can diced green
chilies
1½ Tablespoons chopped chives
mild crackers or raw vegetables
for dipping

Blend cream cheese, butter and liquid from canned shrimp until smooth.
Stir in canned shrimp, fresh shrimp, green chilies and chives. Chill. Serve
with crackers or raw vegetables.

POLYNESIAN GINGER DIP
YIELD: 2 cups

1 cup mayonnaise
1 cup sour cream
¼ cup finely sliced
green onions
¼ cup finely chopped water
chestnuts

¼ cup finely chopped
crystallized ginger
2 cloves garlic, minced
1 Tablespoon soy sauce
dash salt
raw vegetables for dipping or
sesame seed crackers

Combine all ingredients except vegetables for dipping; mix well. Chill.
Serve with raw vegetables or sesame seed crackers.

TORTILLA PINWHEELS
YIELD: 3 dozen

1 4-ounce can diced green
chilies, drained
1 2¼-ounce can chopped
ripe olives, drained
1 2-ounce jar sliced pimiento,
drained

1 8-ounce package cream
cheese, softened
7-10 flour tortillas
salsa (optional)

In a mixing bowl or food processor, combine all ingredients except tortillas.
Spread mixture on each tortilla and roll up jellyroll fashion. Cover with a
damp paper towel and plastic wrap to prevent drying out; chill for several
hours. To serve, slice tortillas into 1-inch segments. If desired, use salsa
as a dipping sauce.

APPETIZERS

MOLDED CHEESE WHEEL

"Great for a cocktail buffet!"

YIELD: 1 9-inch wheel

4 ounces Camembert cheese
  (including rind)
1 cup grated Swiss cheese
4 ounces bleu cheese
3 8-ounce packages cream
  cheese, softened
2 Tablespoons milk

2 Tablespoons sour cream
1¼ cups chopped pecans
4-5 medium apples, cored
  and sliced
2 teaspoons fresh lemon juice
chopped fresh parsley

Line a 9-inch quiche or tart pan with aluminum foil.

Thoroughly combine Camembert, Swiss, bleu and 2 packages of the cream cheese. Set aside.

Beat milk and sour cream into remaining package of cream cheese. Spread in foil-lined pan. Sprinkle with chopped pecans, pressing lightly into surface. Spoon Camembert mixture over nuts and spread to edge. Cover and refrigerate 1-2 days.

To serve, unmold cheese wheel onto platter. Surround with apple slices that have been dipped in 1 cup water mixed with the lemon juice. Sprinkle chopped parsley around the top edge of the wheel.

NOTE: Recipe may be divided into two small wheels.

TEX-MEX DIP

"Like having a mini-taco!"

YIELD: mucho

3 medium avocados
2 Tablespoons fresh lemon juice
½ teaspoon salt
¼ teaspoon pepper
1 teaspoon Worcestershire
  sauce
1 cup sour cream
½ cup mayonnaise
1 1¼-ounce package taco
  seasoning mix

2 10½-ounce cans jalapeño
  bean dip
2 bunches green onions, sliced
3 medium tomatoes, chopped
1 6-ounce can ripe olives, sliced
8 ounces Colby Longhorn
  cheese, grated
tortilla chips

In a bowl, mash avocados with lemon juice, salt, pepper and Worcestershire

In another bowl, mix sour cream, mayonnaise and taco seasoning.

Spread bean dip in a 9 x 13-inch serving dish or a large clear glass bowl. Top with avocado mixture, then sour cream mixture. Layer onions, tomatoes olives and cheese over the sour cream. Chill. Serve with large tortilla chips.

CHILI CON QUESO

"The best!"

YIELD: 6 cups

1 small onion, quartered
2 cloves garlic
1 16-ounce can tomatoes,
  drained
1 4-ounce can diced green chilies
1 Tablespoon Worcestershire
  sauce

1½ pounds Velveeta cheese,
  cubed
8 ounces sharp Cheddar cheese,
  cubed
corn chips

In a blender or food processor, combine onion, garlic, tomatoes, chilies and Worcestershire.

In the top of a double boiler, place tomato mixture; add cheeses. Heat over simmering water until all cheese is melted; stir occasionally. Serve warm with corn chips.

SOUR CREAM FRUIT DIP

"For impromptu gatherings!"

YIELD: 1 cup

1 cup sour cream
2 Tablespoons brown sugar

¼ teaspoon cinnamon
fresh fruit for dipping

Blend all ingredients except fruit. Chill. Serve with a variety of fresh fruit.

VEGETABLE GARDEN DIP

YIELD: 3 cups

1 10-ounce package frozen
  chopped spinach, thawed and
  squeezed dry
1 cup sour cream
1 cup mayonnaise
1 1⅝-ounce package Knorr
  vegetable soup mix

1 8-ounce can water chestnuts,
  drained and chopped
1 small onion, chopped
1 loaf Italian bread or raw
  vegetables for dipping

Thoroughly combine all ingredients except bread and dipping vegetables. Chill. Serve with cubed bread or raw vegetables.

NOTE: For a unique presentation, hollow out a loaf of Italian or other variety bread. Spoon in dip. Cube the removed portion of bread and place around the loaf for dipping.

CHILI DIP

YIELD: 4 cups

1 pound lean ground beef
½ cup chopped onion
½ cup extra hot catsup
1 Tablespoon chili powder
1 teaspoon salt
1 15-ounce can dark red
   kidney beans

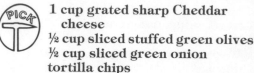

1 cup grated sharp Cheddar
   cheese
½ cup sliced stuffed green olives
½ cup sliced green onion
tortilla chips

In a large skillet, brown beef and onion. Drain grease. Stir in catsup, chili powder, salt and beans; heat thoroughly. Remove to chafing dish. Sprinkle with cheese, olives and onion. Serve warm with tortilla chips.

SALMON CHEESE CANAPES

YIELD: 1 log

"Attractive on a buffet table!"

11 ounces cream cheese,
   softened
¼ cup crumbled bleu cheese
1 teaspoon grated onion
¼ teaspoon hot pepper sauce

1 8-ounce can salmon; drained,
   boned and flaked
1 Tablespoon fresh lemon juice
1 teaspoon horseradish
freshly chopped parsley
1 loaf party rye bread

Beat 3 ounces of the cream cheese with the bleu cheese, onion and pepper sauce. Shape into a 10 inch log. Refrigerate.

Beat the remaining 8 ounces of cream cheese with salmon, lemon juice and horseradish. Pat salmon mixture evenly around outside of the bleu cheese log. Roll the log in parsley and refrigerate overnight. Slice and serve on party rye bread.

BREAST OF PHEASANT

YIELD: What the hunter shoots!

pheasant breasts, boned
beaten egg yolks
fresh bread crumbs

butter
chopped chives
fresh lemon juice

Cut pheasant into bite-size pieces. Place in bowl; cover with beaten egg yolk and marinate for 30 minutes.

Remove pheasant from egg; toss gently in bread crumbs until coated. Place on waxed paper to dry. Season to taste.

In a large skillet, saute pheasant pieces in butter for 3-5 minutes or until lightly browned; remove to a warm oven. After sauteing all the pheasant, remove butter from skillet and film skillet with additional butter. Add chives and a few drops of lemon juice. Drizzle mixture over pheasant. Serve in a napkin-lined basket. Provide wooden picks.

GUACAMOLE

YIELD: 2 cups

3 large ripe avocados
2 small tomatoes, peeled and
  chopped
1 4-ounce can diced
  green chilies

1-1½ Tablespoons
  vegetable oil
1-1½ Tablespoons cider
  vinegar or fresh lemon juice
¾-1 teaspoon salt

Peel, pit and mash avocados. Stir in tomatoes. Add half the chilies and
the smaller quantities of oil, vinegar and salt. Taste. Add additional chilies,
oil, vinegar and salt to taste. Cover surface with plastic wrap; chill until
serving time.

NOTE: Do not make more than several hours in advance or the avocados
will discolor.

TOASTED BUTTER PECANS

YIELD: 3½ cups

3 Tablespoons butter

1 pound pecan halves

In a 10 x 15 x 1-inch baking sheet, melt butter. Place pecans in butter and
stir until well coated. Sprinkle lightly with salt. Bake at 325° for 20-25
minutes, stirring frequently. Drain on paper towels.

MUCHO GRANDE NACHO

SERVES: 16

"Very Mexican!"

1 pound ground beef
1 medium onion, chopped
1 clove garlic, minced
1 4-ounce can diced
  green chilies
1 16-ounce can refried beans
3 cups grated Colby Longhorn
  cheese

⅔ cup picanté sauce
1 cup sliced green onions
1 cup sliced ripe olives
2 cups guacamole (see above)
1 cup sour cream
tortilla chips

In a skillet, saute beef, onion and garlic; drain liquid. Mix in green chilies.

Lightly grease a 9 x 13-inch pan. Spread refried beans in bottom. Top with
meat mixture, then cover with cheese. Drizzle with picanté sauce. Bake at
400° for 20 minutes. Remove from oven. Top with green onions and olives.
Place a large dollop of guacamole at each end of the pan and top all with
dollops of sour cream. Serve with tortilla chips.

NOTE: May also be served as a family entree.

MOZZARELLA VEGETABLE DIP
YIELD: 2 cups

"A different flavor!"

¾ cup sour cream
¾ cup mayonnaise
1½ teaspoons chopped
   fresh parsley
½ teaspoon sugar
½ teaspoon garlic salt

1 Tablespoon grated Parmesan
   cheese
½ cup grated mozzarella cheese
1½ teaspoons minced onion
raw vegetables for dipping

Mix all ingredients except vegetables for dipping. Season to taste. Chill. Serve with raw vegetables.

STUFFED MUSHROOMS
YIELD: 2 dozen

24 bite-size mushrooms,
   cleaned and stems removed

1 3-ounce package cream cheese
6 ounces spicy pork sausage

Stuff mushroom cavity with cream cheese. Top with a small ball of sausage. Broil until sausage is done.

CRABMEAT CHAMPIGNONS
YIELD: 2 dozen

24 large mushrooms
2 Tablespoons freshly grated
   Parmesan cheese
1 8-ounce package cream
   cheese, softened
4 ounces crabmeat
2½ Tablespoons olive oil
2 Tablespoons chopped fresh
   parsley
1½ Tablespoons bread crumbs

2 Tablespoons fresh lemon juice
1½ teaspoons minced shallots
1½ teaspoons Cognac
½ teaspoon Dijon mustard
1 teaspoon salt
½ teaspoon freshly ground
   pepper
fresh parsley sprigs
lemon wedges

Remove mushroom stems; clean caps and set aside to drain. Discard stems. In a mixing bowl, combine all ingredients except mushrooms, parsley and lemon wedges. Beat well.

Fill each mushroom cap with enough of the mixture to form a dome. Place on a lightly greased baking sheet. Bake at 425° for 10-15 minutes. To serve, place mushrooms on a platter and garnish with parsley and lemon wedges.

HOT CHEESE SPREAD
"Quickly made and eaten!"

YIELD: 2 cups

2 cups grated Swiss cheese
¾ cup mayonnaise

2 Tablespoons minced onion
assorted crackers or fresh fruit
  for dipping

Combine all ingredients. Place mixture in a small casserole dish. Bake at
·350° for 15 minutes. Serve with crackers or fresh fruit.

BUFFET MEAT BALLS

YIELD: 6 dozen

¼ cup butter
1 clove garlic, bruised
1½ pounds lean ground beef
¼ cup Italian-style bread crumbs
¼ cup finely chopped walnuts
1 small onion, finely chopped
1 clove garlic, minced
1 Tablespoon grated Parmesan
  cheese

½ teaspoon sweet basil
1 teaspoon salt
dash pepper
⅛ teaspoon paprika
1 egg, lightly beaten
2 rounded Tablespoons
  sour cream
¼ cup red wine

In a large skillet, place butter and bruised garlic clove. Set aside.

In a bowl, combine all remaining ingredients except red wine. Form
mixture into 1-inch balls.

Place skillet over heat and saute garlic in butter for 1 minute. Add meat
balls and brown thoroughly. Add wine to skillet and simmer for 20 minutes.
Discard garlic. Serve in a chafing dish with wooden picks.

SAUCY CHESTNUTS

YIELD: 3 dozen

1 pound lean bacon
2 8-ounce cans whole water
  chestnuts, drained

⅔ cup brown sugar
⅔ cup catsup

Cut bacon strips in half; wrap around water chestnuts and secure with a
wooden pick. Place on a rack over a baking sheet with sides. Bake at
300° for 55 minutes.

Remove from rack and place in a baking dish. Mix sugar and catsup;
pour over bacon. Bake at 300° for 55 minutes, basting occasionally.

CHEESE CRISPIES
"A crunchy treat!"

YIELD: 6 dozen

1 cup butter, softened
2 cups grated sharp Cheddar
  cheese
1 teaspoon salt

2 cups flour
2 cups Rice Krispies
cayenne pepper

In a bowl, thoroughly combine butter, cheese and salt. Add flour, mixing well. Stir in rice cereal. Form dough into ¾-inch balls and flatten with a fork on a baking sheet. Sprinkle very lightly with cayenne. Bake at 375° for 10-12 minutes. Cool.

CURRY DIP

YIELD: 2 cups

2 cups mayonnaise
3 Tablespoons chili sauce
1 Tablespoon curry powder
¼ teaspoon salt
¼ teaspoon pepper

1 Tablespoon garlic powder
1 Tablespoon grated onion
1 Tablespoon Worcestershire
  sauce
raw vegetables for dipping

Combine all ingredients except vegetables for dipping. Chill. Serve with raw vegetables.

MUSHROOM PATÉ
"A preamble for elegant dining!"

YIELD: 1½ cups

8 ounces fresh mushrooms,
  chopped
2 Tablespoons butter
1 8-ounce package cream
  cheese

¾ teaspoon garlic salt
assorted crackers or toasted
  bread rounds

Saute mushrooms in butter for 10-15 minutes until liquid has evaporated. In a blender or food processor, combine mushrooms with cream cheese and garlic salt; blend until smooth. Refrigerate covered for at least 3 hours before serving. Serve with crackers or lightly toasted bread rounds.

CURRY CANAPE

YIELD: 2 dozen

1½ cups grated sharp
  Cheddar cheese
1 cup chopped ripe olives
½ cup sliced green onions

½ cup mayonnaise
1 teaspoon curry powder
1 loaf party rye bread

Combine all ingredients except rye bread.

Place slices of bread on baking sheet and toast under broiler. Turn slices over and spread with mixture. Broil until hot and bubbly.

CANDIED NUTS

YIELD: 1 pound

"A perfect gift!"

1 cup brown sugar
1 teaspoon cinnamon
3 Tablespoons butter
2 Tablespoons water

1 pound pecan or walnut halves
  or a mixture of both
½ cup sugar

In a saucepan, place all ingredients except nuts and white sugar. Bring to a boil. Add nuts, stirring until all liquid is absorbed.

Sprinkle a strip of waxed paper with half of the white sugar. Turn nuts onto the paper. Sprinkle with remaining sugar, stirring until well coated; cool. Shake nuts in a colander to remove excess sugar. Gently separate nuts. Store in an airtight container.

EXTRA-POINT ANTIPASTO

SERVES: 10

"For watching the Super Bowl!"

1 12-ounce bottle chili sauce
⅔ cup catsup
2 Tablespoons fresh lemon juice
2 teaspoons sugar
½ teaspoon garlic powder
2 7-ounce cans water-packed
  tuna, drained
1 8-ounce jar sweet midget
  pickles, chopped

8 ounces fresh mushrooms,
  sliced
1 4-ounce jar stuffed green
  olives, drained
3 medium carrots, peeled and
  thinly sliced
fresh parsley sprigs
crisp crackers

In a bowl, combine chili sauce, catsup, lemon juice, sugar and garlic powder. Add remaining ingredients except parsley and crackers. Refrigerate overnight. Serve decorated with parsley. Pass crackers.

NOTE: Serve the fans this hors d'oeuvre followed by a favorite pasta recipe and salad.

LIPTAUER CHEESE

YIELD: 1 ¼ cups

1 8-ounce package cream
  cheese, softened
¼ cup butter, softened
1 teaspoon capers
1 teaspoon paprika
2 anchovies, chopped

1 shallot, chopped
½ teaspoon caraway seeds
¼ teaspoon salt
dark rye bread
radishes
whole green onions

In a mixing bowl or food processor, combine all ingredients except bread, radishes and onions. Refrigerate overnight. Serve with dark rye bread, radish roses (see page 36) and green onions.

SHRIMP REMOULADE

SERVES: 6

¾ cup mayonnaise
1½ teaspoons horseradish
  mustard
1½ teaspoons capers
1½ teaspoons chopped fresh
  parsley
1½ teaspoons chopped chives

1½ teaspoons chopped sweet
  gherkin pickles
1½ teaspoons tarragon vinegar
1½ pounds medium shrimp;
  cooked, shelled and de-veined
lettuce cups

Combine all ingredients except shrimp and lettuce. Season to taste. Add shrimp. Chill. Serve in lettuce cups as an appetizer.

DEVILISH EGGS AND CAVIAR

YIELD: 20 wedges

"Wickedly delicious!"

10 hard-cooked eggs
¼ cup butter, softened
½ teaspoon celery salt
½ teaspoon dry mustard
1½ Tablespoons minced onion

1 cup sour cream
1 4-ounce jar caviar
fresh parsley
mild crackers (optional)

Peel and chop 9 eggs while still warm. Blend eggs with butter, celery salt, mustard and pepper to taste. Press mixture into 8-inch springform pan that has been chilled.

Combine onion and sour cream. Place on top of egg mixture. Refrigerate for 6 hours.

When ready to serve, remove sides from pan. Cover top with caviar. Peel and finely chop remaining hard-cooked egg and sprinkle over caviar. Garnish with parsley. Serve in individual wedges or with crackers.

SANGRIA

YIELD: 4½ quarts

1 apple, cored and thinly sliced
1 orange, thinly sliced
1 lemon, thinly sliced
1 cup sugar
½ 6-ounce can orange
   juice concentrate

¼ cup fresh lemon juice
2 quarts dry red wine, chilled
1-2 10-ounce bottles club
   soda, chilled
fresh lime or orange wedges

Combine sliced fruits, sugar, orange juice concentrate and lemon juice. Refrigerate overnight.

Combine fruit with wine and soda. To serve, pour into tall glasses filled with ice and garnish with fruit wedges.

HOT BUTTERED RUM

YIELD: 1 quart

"A cold weather warm-up!"

1 cup butter, softened
½ cup brown sugar
½ cup powdered sugar
1 teaspoon nutmeg

1 teaspoon cinnamon
1 pint vanilla ice cream, softened
rum
cinnamon sticks

Cream butter, sugars, nutmeg and cinnamon. Blend in ice cream. Freeze.

To serve, spoon 3-4 tablespoons ice cream mixture into serving mug. Add 3 tablespoons rum and ½-¾ cup boiling water. Stir well. If desired, place a cinnamon stick in each mug.

MINT TEA

YIELD: 2 quarts

"Refreshing as a Colorado breeze!"

1 quart water
12 regular-size tea bags
½ cup fresh mint leaves
1 cup sugar

¼ cup fresh lemon juice
1 6-ounce can frozen orange
   juice concentrate
fresh mint sprigs

In a saucepan, bring water to a boil. Remove from heat, add tea bags and mint leaves. Cover and steep for 1 hour.

In a large pitcher, combine sugar, lemon juice and orange juice concentrate. Remove mint leaves and tea bags from tea, squeezing dry. Add tea mixture to juice mixture. Stir in 3 cups cold water; chill. Serve over ice. Garnish with fresh mint sprigs.

MAGNIFICENT MARGARITAS

SERVES: 1

1½ ounces Tequila
¾ ounce Triple Sec
2 ounces sweet and sour mix

splash of Rose's lime juice
1 lime, cut in half
coarse salt

In a blender, measure Tequila, Triple Sec, sweet and sour mix and lime juice. Add 4 ice cubes and blend until frothy. Rub the rim of a wide-rimmed glass with fresh lime and dip it into coarse salt. Pour drink into glass.

SERVES: 4

6 ounces Tequila
3 ounces Triple Sec
8 ounces sweet and sour mix

½ ounce Rose's lime juice
1 lime, cut in half
coarse salt

Follow same directions as for one, adding 16 ice cubes.

VELVET HAMMER

SERVES: 4

"A smooth drink or dessert!"

1 quart vanilla ice cream
1½ ounces white creme
   de menthe

1 ounce Cointreau
½ ounce Cognac or brandy
½ ounce white creme de cacao

In a blender, combine all ingredients until smooth. Serve in chilled champagne glasses.

NOTE: To serve as a dessert, refreeze mixture. Spoon into dessert cups and garnish with chocolate shavings.

HOT SPICED WINE

YIELD: 4 cups

"After the last ski run!"

3 cups Burgundy wine
1 cup water
1 cup sugar
1 teaspoon whole cloves

3 3-inch sticks of cinnamon
juice of one lemon
juice of one orange

In a saucepan, combine all ingredients. Simmer for 5 minutes. Strain before serving. Serve hot.

SOUPS

LIEUTENANT ZEBULON MONTGOMERY PIKE was
first to officially discover the mountain he called
"Grand Peak" or "Blue Mountain." Pike was in the
region exploring and mapping the Louisiana Purchase
Territory when he made his famous discovery. The
expedition was full of adventure. At one point, when Pike
and his men wandered into Spanish-owned territory, they
were taken prisoners. During this time, all dispatches
were forbidden. When Pike was released and returned
home, he published accounts of his explorations and
adventures which became popular reading both in the
United States and abroad. Pike stated that the mountain,
which would eventually be named for him, would never be
climbed. This statement became a challenge of sorts. Soon
Pikes Peak became a Sunday climb for hikers, troops of
boys, and even hoop-skirted ladies on flower picking
expeditions. Today, an ascent to the top of Pikes Peak is
a must for tourists, marathon runners and auto racers.
Whether you arrive on foot or by car, bus or train, the view
from the top is glorious!

SOUPS

ITALIAN SAUSAGE SOUP
YIELD: 4 quarts
"For après-ski!"

2 pounds link Italian sausage,
sliced ½ inch thick
2 cloves garlic, minced
2 medium onions, chopped
1 28-ounce can tomatoes,
chopped
4 10½-ounce cans beef broth
¾ cup dry red wine

¾ cup water
¾ teaspoon sweet basil
3 Tablespoons chopped
fresh parsley
1 green pepper, chopped
3 medium zucchini,
sliced ¼ inch thick
5 ounces bow tie noodles

In a large kettle or Dutch oven, brown sausage and drain. Add garlic
and onions; cook until soft. Add tomatoes with juice, broth, wine, water
and basil. Simmer for 30 minutes. Cool and refrigerate overnight.

One hour before serving, de-grease soup. Reheat soup, adding parsley,
green pepper, zucchini and noodles. Simmer covered for 15 minutes
or until noodles are tender.

STRAWBERRY SOUP
YIELD: 1 quart
"Refreshingly versatile!"

1½ cups water
¾ cup Taylor Lake
Country Red wine
½ cup sugar
2 Tablespoons fresh lemon juice
1 3-inch stick of cinnamon

1 quart strawberries,
hulled and pureed
½ cup heavy cream
¼ cup sour cream
1 lime, thinly sliced

In a large saucepan, bring water, wine, sugar, lemon juice and cinnamon
stick to a boil. Boil gently for 15 minutes, stirring occasionally. Add
strawberry puree and simmer for 10 minutes. Discard cinnamon stick
and chill.

At serving time, whip cream stiff. Combine with sour cream and fold
into soup. Garnish each serving with a slice of lime.

NOTE: Great as part of a luncheon, the first course of a summer dinner
or a light dessert.

CREAM OF ASPARAGUS SOUP

YIELD: 2½ quarts

15 fresh asparagus spears
1 cup chopped onion
1 cup sliced leek
¼ cup butter
4 medium potatoes,
  peeled and chopped

5½ cups chicken stock
  or broth
1 teaspoon salt
¼ teaspoon white pepper
1 cup heavy cream

Peel and wash asparagus spears. Cut stalks into quarters, reserving the tips for garnish.

In a large saucepan, saute onion and leek in butter. Cook for 2 minutes and add asparagus stalks. Cook for 3 minutes. Add potatoes, 5 cups of the chicken stock, salt and pepper. Bring to a boil and simmer covered for 45 minutes.

Prepare asparagus tips by cooking for 2 minutes in the remaining ½ cup stock. Remove tips from stock and set aside for garnish. Add stock to soup.

Cool soup slightly and puree it in small amounts. Return to heat, add cream and adjust seasonings. Serve garnished with asparagus tips.

GAZPACHO

YIELD: 2½ quarts

"With a southwestern flair!"

2 cloves garlic
1 28-ounce can
  stewed tomatoes
2 teaspoons snipped
  fresh chives
1 Tablespoon chopped
  fresh parsley
1 Tablespoon Worcestershire
  sauce
1½ teaspoons salt
½ teaspoon freshly ground
  black pepper

2 teaspoons olive oil
2 teaspoons fresh lemon juice
few dashes Tabasco sauce
1 Tablespoon sugar
4½ cups tomato juice
1½ cups sliced celery
1 cucumber; peeled, seeded
  and diced
1 cup peeled, chopped
  fresh tomato
½ cup chopped green pepper
¼ cup chopped onion

In a blender or food processor, puree garlic with stewed tomatoes. Transfer to a large storage container; stir in remaining ingredients. Refrigerate for 5 hours. Serve cold.

OYSTER-SHRIMP GUMBO

YIELD: 2½ quarts

1 large onion, chopped
2 cloves garlic, minced
½ green pepper, chopped
¼ cup butter
2 Tablespoons vegetable oil
1 28-ounce can tomatoes
2 16-ounce cans okra
3 Tablespoons flour
1 quart water
2 chicken bouillon cubes
1 teaspoon salt

1 teaspoon pepper
1 6-ounce bottle clam juice
1 pound medium shrimp, peeled
½ pint fresh oysters with juice
2 Tablespoons fresh lemon juice
1 teaspoon Pickapeppa sauce
1 Tablespoon Worcestershire
  sauce
1 Tablespoon gumbo filé
2 Tablespoons sherry

In a saucepan, saute onion, garlic and green pepper in 2 tablespoons butter and oil until soft. Add tomatoes and crush. Add okra.

In a large kettle or Dutch oven, melt 2 tablespoons butter. Whisk in flour; cook for 2 minutes. Gradually add water; stir in bouillon cubes, salt, pepper and clam juice. Add sauteed vegetables. Cook covered for 1 hour. Add shrimp, oysters with juice, lemon juice, Pickapeppa sauce and Worcestershire. Cook for 5 minutes. Add gumbo filé and sherry. Cook for 2 minutes.

FRUKTSOPPA

YIELD: 2½ quarts

"A fruit soup for brunch!"

8 ounces pitted prunes
1 cup golden raisins
8 ounces dried apricots
2 quarts cold water
1 cup sugar
1 3-inch stick of cinnamon

3 Tablespoons tapioca
1-2 teaspoons Angostura
  Bitters
6 thin orange slices
6 thin lemon slices
1 cup sour cream

In a large saucepan, place dried fruits. Pour cold water over fruit and let soak for 1 hour. Add sugar and cinnamon. Cover and cook slowly for 1 hour.

Soften tapioca in ½ cup cold water for 5 minutes. Add the tapioca and bitters to soup. Cook slowly for 10 minutes or until soup clears. Remove from heat; add orange and lemon slices. Serve chilled with a dollop of sour cream.

CREAMY CLAM CHOWDER

YIELD: 2 quarts

12 ounces minced clams
 with juice
1 cup chopped onion
1 cup sliced celery
1 cup peeled, diced potatoes
¾ cup butter

½ cup flour
1 quart half-and-half
2 teaspoons sugar
1½ teaspoons salt
white pepper

In a 2½-quart saucepan, combine clams with juice, onion, celery and potatoes. Barely cover with water; simmer covered until potatoes are tender.

In a large saucepan, melt butter; add flour and cook for 2 minutes. Whisk in half-and-half; cook until thickened. Add undrained vegetables, sugar, salt and pepper. Simmer for 3 minutes.

CREAMY CHICKEN AND
GREEN VEGETABLE SOUP

YIELD: 3½ cups

"Tastes like homemade!"

1 10¾-ounce can cream
 of chicken soup
1 15-ounce can chicken broth

½ cup frozen chopped
 broccoli, spinach or
 asparagus
¾ cup heavy cream

In a blender or food processor, combine all ingredients. Pour mixture into a saucepan; simmer for 20 minutes. Serve hot or cold.

CRAB AND SPINACH SOUP

YIELD: 2 quarts

½ cup chopped onion
1 cup sliced celery
3 Tablespoons butter
2 Tablespoons flour
1 14½-ounce can
 chicken broth
2 cups half-and-half

½ teaspoon salt
⅛ teaspoon white pepper
⅛ teaspoon nutmeg
1 6½-ounce can crabmeat
1 10-ounce package frozen
 chopped spinach, thawed
 and squeezed dry

In a large saucepan, saute onion and celery in butter until soft. Stir in flour; cook for 2 minutes. Whisk in broth; cook until thickened. Over low heat, stir in half-and-half, seasonings, crab and spinach.

TOMATO SOUP OLÉ
"South-of-the-border snappy!"

YIELD: 5 cups

2 ½ Tablespoons butter
1 ½ Tablespoons flour
2 cups milk
2 ½ cups tomato sauce
1 4-ounce can salsa
1 28-ounce can tomatoes
1 small onion, chopped

1 bay leaf
1 teaspoon salt
¼ teaspoon pepper
¼ teaspoon Worcestershire
  sauce
1 cup sour cream

In a saucepan, combine butter and flour to make a roux. Cook for
2 minutes. Whisk in milk, stirring until thickened.

In another saucepan, combine tomato sauce, salsa, tomatoes, onion and
bay leaf. Simmer for 5 minutes, stirring to break up tomatoes.

Thoroughly combine milk and tomato mixtures. Stir in salt, pepper and
Worcestershire. Serve hot or cold with a dollop of sour cream.

BEAN AND SAUSAGE SOUP
"Great for football Sundays!"

YIELD: 1 ½ quarts

1 pound bulk hot pork sausage
1 16-ounce can dark red
  kidney beans
1 16-ounce can tomatoes
2 cups water
1 medium onion,
  chopped
1 medium potato,
  peeled and cubed

1 medium green pepper,
  chopped
1 bay leaf
¼ teaspoon garlic salt
¼ teaspoon thyme
⅛ teaspoon pepper

In a kettle or Dutch oven, brown sausage and drain well. Add remaining
ingredients. Simmer covered for approximately 1 hour.

GOLDEN GLORY CHOWDER

YIELD: 3 quarts

8 ounces bacon, sliced
1 cup chopped onion
½ green pepper, chopped
3 cups water
1 14-ounce can chicken broth
5 cups peeled, cubed potatoes

4 cups fresh or canned
whole kernel corn, drained
1 4-ounce jar chopped pimiento
1½ cups half-and-half
2 teaspoons salt
1 teaspoon pepper

In a kettle, fry bacon until crisp; pour off most of the bacon fat. Add onion and green pepper; cook until tender. Stir in water and broth; bring to a boil. Add potatoes and cook slowly for 15 minutes or until potatoes are tender. Add corn, pimiento, half-and-half and seasonings. Cook gently for 5 minutes.

SEAFOOD CHOWDER

YIELD: 2 quarts

"Velvety!"

¼-cup butter
½ cup finely minced onion
2 cups chicken stock or broth
1½ cups sliced celery
1½ cups peeled, thinly sliced
carrots
1 teaspoon salt
dash pepper
½ bay leaf
pinch of thyme

8 ounces white fish fillets
3 cups milk
¼ cup flour
1 cup heavy cream
1 6-ounce package frozen
crabmeat, thawed and drained
1 6½-ounce can minced clams
with juice
finely minced fresh parsley

In a large saucepan, melt butter and saute onion. Add chicken stock, celery, carrots, salt, pepper, bay leaf and thyme. Simmer for 20 minutes or until vegetables are tender.

Cut fish into bite-size pieces and add to soup.

Add 1 cup of the milk to the flour to make a thin paste. Add paste to hot mixture, stirring constantly; cook until thickened. Add remaining milk gradually, stirring gently. Add cream, crabmeat and clams with juice. Heat, but do not boil. Serve garnished with minced parsley.

NOTE: For a flavor variation, add 1 tablespoon fresh lemon juice or ¼ cup dry sherry to soup before serving.

MULLIGATAWNY SOUP
YIELD: 2½ quarts
"Flavorful curried chicken and tomato soup!"

3 whole chicken breasts,
  split and skinned
¼ cup flour
¼ cup butter
1 small onion, chopped
½ green pepper, chopped
2 medium carrots,
  peeled and sliced
2 tart apples; peeled, cored
  and chopped

2 Tablespoons chopped
  fresh parsley
1 teaspoon salt
¼ teaspoon pepper
2 teaspoons curry powder
¼ teaspoon nutmeg
2 whole cloves
1 28-ounce can tomatoes
1 quart water

Dredge chicken in flour. In a skillet, brown chicken in butter.

In a large kettle or Dutch oven, combine remaining ingredients with chicken and simmer for 1½ hours. Remove chicken and bone. Cut chicken into small pieces and return to soup mixture. Refrigerate overnight.

Before serving, de-grease soup; reheat and season to taste.

CREAM OF BROCCOLI SOUP
YIELD: 2 quarts

1½ pounds fresh broccoli
3 Tablespoons butter
1 cup chopped onion
½ cup sliced celery
½ cup chopped leek

1 clove garlic, minced
6 cups chicken stock or broth
1½ cups heavy cream
4 ounces processed American
  cheese

Rinse and trim broccoli. Cut into pieces, discarding the woody stems.

In a large saucepan, melt butter. Saute onion, celery, leek and garlic for 5 minutes. Add broccoli and chicken stock. Bring to a boil; cover and simmer for 30 minutes.

Puree soup. Return to saucepan; add cream and cheese. Stir until cheese is melted. Season to taste.

COLD AVOCADO SOUP

YIELD: 2 quarts

"Rich and tasty!"

3 cups chicken stock or broth
4 avocados, peeled and pitted
½ cup picanté sauce
½ cup chopped onion
juice of ½ lemon

¼ teaspoon garlic salt
2 cups heavy cream
fresh parsley sprigs
nacho-flavored tortilla chips

In a blender or food processor, combine all ingredients except cream, parsley and chips. Stir in cream and season to taste. Chill. Garnish individual servings with a sprig of parsley and a whole tortilla chip placed in the center of the soup.

NOTE: Color of soup may darken if made more than 1 hour in advance.

SIMPLY SUMMER SOUP

YIELD: 1 quart

1 cup cucumber puree
12 ounces plain yogurt
2 Tablespoons minced onion
¼ cup chili sauce
¾ teaspoon salt
1 cup chicken stock or broth
1 Tablespoon olive oil
1 small onion, chopped

1 small green pepper, chopped
1 cucumber; peeled, seeded
   and chopped
1 tomato, chopped
1 cup sour cream
2 teaspoons snipped
   fresh chives

Peel, seed and puree enough cucumber to make 1 cup.

Blend puree with yogurt, minced onion, chili sauce, salt, chicken stock and oil. Chill.

When ready to serve, add remaining vegetables. Garnish soup with a dollop of sour cream and sprinkle with chives.

POTATO SOUP

"A hearty winter soup!"

5 strips bacon, sliced
5 Tablespoons butter
½ cup flour
1 quart whole milk
1 Tablespoon salt
1 teaspoon white pepper
6 medium potatoes,
    peeled and cubed

1 medium onion, chopped
½ teaspoon Worcestershire
    sauce
¼ teaspoon paprika
chopped fresh parsley
    or chives

In a large saucepan, saute bacon in butter for 3 minutes. Stir in flour and cook for 2 minutes. Whisk in milk, salt and pepper. Simmer for 5 minutes.

In another saucepan, cook potatoes and onion in just enough water to cover. When vegetables are tender, transfer them with water to the milk mixture. Add Worcestershire, paprika and additional milk if soup is too thick. Simmer for 5 minutes. Serve garnished with fresh parsley or chives.

CHEESY ZUCCHINI SOUP

4 strips bacon, sliced
½ cup chopped green onion
¼ cup chopped green pepper
2½ cups quartered,
    sliced zucchini
1 Tablespoon chopped pimiento
1½ teaspoons salt
1 cup water

¼ cup butter
¼ cup flour
2½ cups milk
½ teaspoon pepper
½ teaspoon Worcestershire
    sauce
1 cup grated mild
    Cheddar cheese

In a skillet, fry bacon. Add onion and green pepper; saute in bacon fat. Add zucchini, pimiento, ½ teaspoon salt and water. Cover and simmer for 10 minutes.

In a large saucepan, melt butter. Whisk in flour; cook for 2 minutes. Whisk in milk, 1 teaspoon salt, pepper and Worcestershire sauce. Stir in cheese, cooking until melted. Stir in zucchini mixture.

VICHYSSOISE

YIELD: 2½ quarts

"A classic!"

3 large leeks
¼ cup butter
2½ pounds potatoes,
  peeled and thinly sliced
3 cups chicken stock or broth
dash freshly grated nutmeg

2 cups milk
2 cups half-and-half
2 teaspoons salt
dash white pepper
snipped fresh chives
fresh lemon wedges

With a sharp knife, slit leeks lengthwise to within one-half inch of the root. Under cold water, separate to thoroughly remove dirt. Discard root tip and green part; thinly slice remaining white part.

In a saucepan, cook leeks in butter until tender but not brown. Add potatoes, chicken stock and nutmeg. Cook for 30 minutes or until potatoes are tender. In a blender or food processor, blend soup until smooth. Place mixture in a large storage container. Add milk, half-and-half, salt and pepper. Cover and chill.

Before serving, adjust seasonings; thin if necessary. Serve soup cold, topped with chives and a wedge of lemon on the side.

MINESTRONE SOUP

YIELD: 4 quarts

1 clove garlic, minced
1 cup chopped onion
1 cup sliced celery
¼ cup vegetable oil
1 12-ounce can tomato paste
1 10-ounce can beef broth
2½ quarts water
1 cup chopped cabbage
1 10-ounce package frozen
  mixed vegetables

2½ teaspoons salt
¼ teaspoon pepper
½ teaspoon rosemary
1 pound lean ground beef
1 15-ounce can dark red
  kidney beans
1 cup elbow macaroni
4 ounces Colby Longhorn
  cheese, grated

In a large kettle or Dutch oven, saute garlic, onion and celery in oil for 3 minutes.

Add tomato paste, beef broth, water, cabbage, frozen vegetables, salt, pepper and rosemary. Bring to a boil. Add ground beef in small balls. Cover and simmer for 1 hour. Add kidney beans and elbow macaroni. Simmer for 15 minutes or until macaroni is tender. Serve hot, sprinkled with grated cheese.

SALADS AND DRESSINGS

GENERAL WILLIAM JACKSON PALMER founded
Colorado Springs, nicknamed "Little London" by the
English residents, at the foot of majestic Pikes Peak as a
future home for his new wife, "Queen" Mellen. Palmer
loved the surroundings of the Pikes Peak region, and he
dreamed of founding a city which would rival the great
resort spas of Europe. It was to be a special place with
wide streets and open spaces for parks. It would also be
one of the stops on his Denver and Rio Grande Railroad.
Palmer's heart belonged to Glen Eyrie (Nest of Eagles).
He built the three-story, wood-sided home in 1871
for "Queen." Intimidated by the realities of the primitive
western lifestyle, "Queen" spent much time apart from
Palmer. After 13 years of marriage, she left for more
civilized climes, finally establishing herself in London.
After her death, Palmer constructed the present Glen Eyrie,
a castle-like structure near the Garden of the Gods.
Designed by the Denver architect, Frederic Sterner, it
contains hundreds of pieces of rock which were brought
from the Colorado mountains to give the exterior of the
structure an "old" appearance. The roof was from Europe
as was the ornamental stone for the 40 fireplaces and
the Chippendale furniture. It was a fabulous home for
Palmer and his daughters in the Colorado mountains
he loved.

SALADS AND DRESSINGS

*Found elsewhere in the book.

ORANGE AMBROSIA
YIELD: 1¾ cups
"Food for the gods!"

1 cup white grape juice
½ cup orange marmalade
¼ cup Grand Marnier

fresh fruit, canned Mandarin
  oranges and pineapple chunks
fresh mint sprigs

In a jar, combine all ingredients except fruit and mint; shake well. Pour over a variety of fruits. Chill ambrosia. Bananas, if desired, should be added just before serving.

Serve in a wide-rimmed champagne glass garnished with a sprig of mint. Guests eat the fruit and sip the remaining nectar.

GREEN GRAPES ELEGANT
SERVES: 6

½ cup sour cream
3 Tablespoons brown sugar

1½ pounds seedless green
  grapes

Thoroughly combine sour cream and sugar. Stir in grapes. Refrigerate for 4 hours or longer.

NOTE: By adding 1½ tablespoons brandy, this becomes a special dessert.

GOOSEBERRY-ORANGE MOLD
SERVES: 9

1 16-ounce can gooseberries
1 3-ounce package lemon
  gelatin
¼ cup sugar

1 cup orange juice
¾ cup sliced celery
¼ cup chopped pecans

Drain gooseberries, reserving gooseberry juice. Add enough water to juice to measure ¾ cup.

In a saucepan, combine gooseberry juice, sugar and gelatin. Bring to a boil, stirring to dissolve. Remove from heat. Add orange juice. Pour into an 8-inch square pan; chill until partially set. Stir in celery, gooseberries and pecans. Chill until firm.

FROSTY CRANBERRY SALAD

SERVES: 12

1 8-ounce can crushed
  pineapple
1 6-ounce package raspberry
  gelatin
1 8-ounce package cream
  cheese, softened

2 Tablespoons mayonnaise
1 cup heavy cream, whipped
½ cup chopped walnuts
1 tart apple, peeled and chopped
1 16-ounce can whole berry
  cranberry sauce

Drain pineapple; reserve liquid. Add enough water to pineapple juice to make 2 cups; bring to a boil. Dissolve gelatin in boiling liquid. Chill until partially set.

Beat cream cheese and mayonnaise until fluffy; gradually add gelatin mixture. Fold in whipped cream. Add pineapple, nuts, apple and cranberries. Pour into oiled Bundt pan or 9 x 13-inch serving dish. Chill.

CRANBERRY DELIGHT

SERVES: 8

2 cups chopped fresh
  cranberries
½ cup sugar·
2 cups red grapes, seeded
  and halved

2 cups miniature marshmallows
½ cup chopped pecans
1 cup heavy cream, whipped

Combine cranberries and sugar. Refrigerate overnight.

Drain and discard cranberry juice. Fold in remaining ingredients. Chill.

APPLE CIDER MOLD

SERVES: 9

2 envelopes unflavored gelatin
3 cups apple cider
6 Tablespoons sugar
⅛ teaspoon salt

½ cup peeled and diced apple
½ cup chopped raw cranberries
½ cup thinly sliced celery
sour cream or whipped cream

In a saucepan, sprinkle gelatin on cider. Bring to a boil. Add sugar and salt, stirring until dissolved. Chill until syrupy.

Fold in apple, cranberries and celery. Turn into individual molds or an 8-inch square pan. Chill until firm. Garnish with a dollop of sour cream or whipped cream.

BOUQUET SALAD

SERVES: 10

Italian Vinaigrette Dressing

¼ cup tarragon vinegar
1½ teaspoons salt
1 Tablespoon sugar
1 Tablespoon Italian herb
  seasoning

¼ teaspoon Tabasco sauce
½ cup vegetable oil
2 Tablespoons minced fresh
  parsley

In a jar, combine dressing ingredients; shake well.

Salad

1 16-ounce can cut green beans
1 15-ounce can dark red kidney
  beans
1 6-ounce can pitted ripe olives
1 2-ounce jar chopped pimientos

1 6-ounce jar marinated
  artichokes
1½ cups sliced celery
4 ounces fresh mushrooms,
  sliced
1 medium onion, sliced

Drain vegetables. Combine with celery, mushrooms and onions. Pour dressing over salad and marinate in refrigerator overnight.

TANGY GREEN BEAN SALAD

SERVES: 6

Horseradish Salad Dressing

½ cup sour cream
¼ cup mayonnaise
½ teaspoon fresh lemon juice
⅛ teaspoon dry mustard

1½ teaspoons horseradish
¼ teaspoon fresh onion juice
1 teaspoon snipped fresh chives
cracked black pepper

Combine dressing ingredients. Chill.

Salad

1 28-ounce can cut green beans,
  drained
½ small onion, thinly sliced

1 Tablespoon vegetable oil
1 Tablespoon cider vinegar

In a bowl, combine green beans and onion. Sprinkle with oil, vinegar, salt and pepper. Chill.

When ready to serve, drain vegetables and toss with enough dressing to coat generously.

NOTE: Dressing is also delicious on sliced cucumbers.

HOT GERMAN POTATO SALAD
SERVES: 8

"Good with bratwurst!"

½ pound bacon, cut into ½-inch
  pieces
¼ cup white vinegar mixed
  with ¼ cup water
1 egg, beaten

1 teaspoon sugar
1 teaspoon salt
¼ teaspoon pepper
½ cup chopped onion
5 cups cooked, sliced potatoes

Fry and drain bacon. Reserve and cool drippings. Add vinegar-water mixture, egg, sugar, salt, pepper and onion to drippings. Cook over low heat until thickened. Stir in potatoes and bacon. Serve warm.

POTATO SALAD
SERVES: 6-8

"Most popular for picnics!"

1 cup mayonnaise
½ cup sour cream
1 Tablespoon prepared mustard
½ cup sweet pickle relish
1 teaspoon salt

6 potatoes; cooked, peeled
  and diced
¼ cup chopped onion
4 hard-cooked eggs, chopped
1½ cups sliced celery

Combine mayonnaise, sour cream, mustard, pickle relish and salt. Mix with remaining ingredients. Adjust seasonings and chill.

CARROT COPPER PENNIES
SERVES: 8

1½ pounds carrots, peeled
  and sliced ⅛ inch thick
6 Tablespoons cider vinegar
⅓ cup sugar
¼ cup vegetable oil
1 teaspoon prepared mustard
1 teaspoon Worcestershire
  sauce

½ teaspoon salt
1 8-ounce can tomato sauce
1 medium onion, quartered and
  thinly sliced
½ green pepper, sliced ⅛ inch
  thick and 1½ inches long
lettuce

Steam carrots until tender-crisp.

In a bowl, combine vinegar, sugar, oil, mustard, Worcestershire, salt and tomato sauce. Add carrots, onion and green pepper; stir to coat. Refrigerate overnight. Serve by removing vegetables from sauce and mounding onto lettuce.

WHITE CORN SALAD

SERVES: 6

"Colorful!"

Dressing

¼ cup sour cream
1 Tablespoon white vinegar
¼ teaspoon dry mustard

1 Tablespoon mayonnaise
¼ teaspoon pepper
½ teaspoon salt

Salad

1 12-ounce can shoe peg white
   corn, drained
¼ cup chopped red onion
2 Tablespoons chopped green
   pepper

½ cup peeled, seeded and
   chopped cucumber
1 cup chopped tomato

In a large bowl, combine all dressing ingredients. Stir in vegetables. Chill.

LIMA BEANS AND WATER CHESTNUTS

SERVES: 6

1 10-ounce package frozen baby
   lima beans
1 8-ounce can sliced water
   chestnuts, drained

½ cup prepared Italian
   salad dressing
1 teaspoon dill weed
lettuce cups

Cook beans until tender-crisp. Combine with remaining ingredients except
lettuce cups. Cover and chill. Serve in lettuce cups.

GREEN AND WHITE SALAD

SERVES: 8

1 small bunch broccoli
1 small head cauliflower
1 teaspoon fresh lemon juice
1 teaspoon dill weed
1 cup mayonnaise

¼ cup chopped onion
1½ cups sliced celery
1 2-ounce jar stuffed green
   olives, sliced
3 hard-cooked eggs, chopped

Wash and cut broccoli and cauliflower into flowerets. Steam until tender-
crisp. Drain and chill.

In a large bowl, combine lemon juice, dill weed and mayonnaise. Add
vegetables and eggs, tossing gently. Season to taste. Refrigerate overnight.

SALADS

COLORFUL CAULIFLOWER SALAD   SERVES: 8

Dressing

½ cup vegetable oil
3 Tablespoons fresh lemon juice
3 Tablespoons red wine vinegar
1 teaspoon salt

½ teaspoon sugar
¼ teaspoon freshly ground
   black pepper

Salad

4 cups thinly sliced raw
   cauliflower flowerets
1 cup coarsely chopped ripe
   olives
⅔ cup chopped green pepper

½ cup chopped pimiento
½ cup thinly sliced red or green
   onion
salad greens

In a blender or food processor, combine all dressing ingredients. Pour over vegetables except salad greens; toss lightly. Cover and refrigerate for 5 hours or overnight. Serve salad in a bowl lined with salad greens.

PENROSE APPLE SALAD   SERVES: 6

Dressing

¼ cup red wine vinegar
¼ cup vegetable oil

½ teaspoon salt
¼ teaspoon pepper

In a jar, vigorously shake dressing ingredients.

Salad

1 clove garlic
1 small head cauliflower,
   thinly sliced
1 cup sliced celery

3 green onions, sliced
¾ cup chopped fresh parsley
3 red apples, cored and cubed

Rub a salad bowl with cut edges of garlic clove; discard garlic. Place cauliflower, celery, onions and parsley in salad bowl. Toss lightly with dressing. Refrigerate for 2-3 hours. Add apples just before serving.

CELERY-MUSHROOM VINAIGRETTE   SERVES: 6
"From our friend Carol Truax!"

¼ cup olive oil
1 Tablespoon fresh lemon juice
½ teaspoon salt
⅛ teaspoon pepper

8 ounces celery, thinly sliced
8 ounces fresh mushroom caps,
   thinly sliced
salad greens

Combine oil, lemon juice, salt and pepper. Pour over celery and mushrooms. Chill. Serve on salad greens.

NOTE: For a variation, add any fresh or dried herbs to this salad.

34

FRED HARVEY SLAW

SERVES: 6

Dressing

1 teaspoon sugar
1½ teaspoons salt
½ teaspoon dry mustard

½ teaspoon celery seed
½ cup vegetable oil
½ cup cider vinegar

In a saucepan, whisk dressing ingredients. Place over low heat; boil for 1 minute. Allow to cool while preparing slaw.

Slaw

1 medium head cabbage,
  shredded
1 small onion, diced

1 carrot, peeled and grated
½ cup sugar

Combine slaw ingredients. Stir in dressing; cover and refrigerate for at least 4 hours. Toss occasionally.

NOTE: Best when prepared a day in advance. Will keep in the refrigerator for at least a week.

TOMATO MOLD WITH CUCUMBER DRESSING

SERVES: 6

Tomato Mold

1 3-ounce package lemon
  gelatin
1 cup water

1 16-ounce can stewed tomatoes,
  pureed

In a saucepan, bring salad ingredients to a boil, stirring to dissolve gelatin. Pour into a mold and chill until set. Unmold and garnish with dressing.

Cucumber-Curry Dressing

⅔ cup mayonnaise
2 Tablespoons milk
½ teaspoon curry powder

½ cucumber; peeled, seeded and
  diced

Combine dressing ingredients; chill.

MUSTARD RING

SERVES: 10

"For a New Year's buffet!"

4 eggs
1 cup water
½ cup cider vinegar
¾ cup sugar
1 envelope unflavored gelatin

1½ Tablespoons dry mustard
½ teaspoon turmeric
¼ teaspoon salt
1 cup heavy cream, whipped
chutney or cole slaw

In the top of a double boiler, combine eggs, water, vinegar, sugar, gelatin, mustard, turmeric and salt. Place over simmering water; whisk until thickened. Cool.

Fold in whipped cream. Turn into a 1½-quart ring mold. Chill. Unmold and serve with the center filled with chutney or cole slaw.

TRICOLOR ASPIC

SERVES: 8

Tomato Stock

12 ounces V-8 juice
1 teaspoon celery salt
1 bay leaf
1 16-ounce can stewed tomatoes
juice of ½ lemon

1 Tablespoon sugar
1 teaspoon Worcestershire
  sauce
dash Tabasco sauce

In a large saucepan, combine all stock ingredients and simmer for 30 minutes. Strain.

Layer I

2 envelopes unflavored gelatin   1 cup sliced celery

Dissolve gelatin in 2 cups of the hot tomato stock. Stir in celery and pour into a 1½-quart mold. Chill until firm.

Layer II

2 medium avocados
½ teaspoon salt
1 Tablespoon fresh lemon juice

1 teaspoon Worcestershire
  sauce
1 package unflavored gelatin
1 cup hot water

Puree avocado with salt, lemon juice and Worcestershire. Dissolve gelatin in hot water. Combine avocado mixture with gelatin. Pour over tomato mixture; chill until firm.

Layer III

1 package unflavored gelatin
¼ cup hot water

1 cup sour cream
fresh lettuce

Dissolve gelatin in hot water. Stir in sour cream. Pour over avocado mixture; chill until firm. To serve, unmold onto fresh lettuce.

To make radish roses, score the peel of a radish at equal distances from top to bottom eight times. Starting at the top, loosen the peel of each section most of the way down. Place in cold water so that the radish may "flower."

ORANGE-SPINACH SALAD WITH HONEY-MUSTARD DRESSING

SERVES: 6

Honey-Mustard Dressing

¾ cup safflower oil
¼ cup red wine vinegar
¼ cup honey
¼ cup Dijon mustard
¼ cup sesame seeds, toasted

2 cloves garlic, minced
½ teaspoon freshly ground
  pepper
½ teaspoon salt

Combine dressing ingredients; mix well. Chill.

Salad

10 ounces fresh spinach
2 large oranges, peeled
  and sectioned

1 small red onion, thinly sliced
8 ounces bacon, cooked
  and crumbled

Wash, stem and dry spinach. Tear into pieces. Add orange and onion.
To serve, toss salad with enough dressing to coat; sprinkle with bacon.

SPINACH SALAD

SERVES: 6

"An old favorite!"

Dressing

¼ cup sugar
½ teaspoon salt
½ teaspoon celery salt
1 teaspoon pepper
1 teaspoon dry mustard
1 teaspoon Worcestershire
  sauce

⅓ cup cider vinegar
1 cup vegetable oil
½ cup catsup
2 green onions, chopped
1 clove garlic, bruised

In a pint jar, combine all dressing ingredients; shake well. Chill. Remove
garlic clove and serve desired amount of dressing over salad.

Salad

8 ounces fresh spinach
2 hard-cooked eggs, diced

6 strips bacon, cooked and
  crumbled

Wash spinach; remove stems and dry spinach. Tear into pieces and place
in a large bowl. Add eggs, bacon and dressing; toss gently.

GARDEN OF THE GODS SALAD

SERVES: 6

Vinaigrette Dressing

½ cup olive oil
¼ cup white wine vinegar
¼ cup sliced green onions
¼ cup minced fresh parsley
1 teaspoon sugar

1 teaspoon salt
1 teaspoon dry mustard
⅛ teaspoon black or cayenne
   pepper

Salad

1 large head romaine lettuce,
   torn

8 ounces fresh mushrooms,
   thinly sliced

In a blender or food processor, combine dressing ingredients and chill. To serve, toss dressing with lettuce and mushrooms.

CHATEAU SALAD

SERVES: 4

"Good with tomato-base dishes!"

Tomato Vinaigrette Dressing

¼ cup safflower oil
3 Tablespoons tomato juice
1 Tablespoon fresh lemon juice
2 teaspoons grated onion

¼ teaspoon salt
¼ teaspoon pepper
¼ teaspoon sugar
¼ teaspoon sweet basil

In a jar, shake dressing ingredients. Let stand while preparing salad.

Salad

⅓ cup walnuts, coarsely broken
1 head Boston bibb lettuce, torn

¼ cup grated Parmesan cheese

In a 400° oven, lightly toast walnuts for 3-5 minutes.

In a large salad bowl, place lettuce, walnuts and cheese. Toss with dressing.

To flute a mushroom, draw a citrus stripper across the mushroom from the center to the edge. Space cuts ¼ inch apart at the edge.

ORIENTAL CHICKEN SALAD

SERVES: 6

"For a light meal!"

Dressing

2 Tablespoons sugar
1 teaspoon salt
½ teaspoon pepper

3 Tablespoons white vinegar
¼ cup vegetable oil

In a jar, shake dressing ingredients.

Salad

2 ounces bean thread
3 Tablespoons slivered almonds,
    lightly toasted
3 Tablespoons sesame seeds,
    lightly toasted

1 pound white chicken meat,
    cooked and very thinly sliced
1 small head iceberg lettuce,
    thinly sliced
4 green onions, sliced

Fry small amounts of bean thread in oil for 3-4 seconds, or until they have expanded. Drain on paper towel.

In a large bowl, place all ingredients. Pour on dressing and toss lightly.

NOTE: Won ton skins may be substituted for bean thread. Cut 12 won ton skins into 4 strips each. Fry strips in hot oil until golden brown. Drain on paper towels.

ROYAL TURKEY SALAD

SERVES: 6

"A different kind of Caesar!"

French Vinaigrette Dressing

¼ cup vegetable oil
¼ cup olive oil
3 Tablespoons white wine
    vinegar
1 teaspoon dry mustard
1 teaspoon fresh lemon juice

½ teaspoon salt
½ teaspoon Worcestershire
    sauce
⅛ teaspoon freshly ground
    black pepper

Thoroughly combine all dressing ingredients. Chill.

Salad

1 head romaine lettuce, torn
3 cups cooked, cubed turkey
3 Tablespoons grated Parmesan
    cheese

⅓ cup slivered almonds, toasted
1 cup croutons

Combine salad ingredients; toss lightly with dressing.

SALADS

SUMMER SALAD WITH RASPBERRY MAYONNAISE
SERVES: 8

"Sumptuous!"

Raspberry Mayonnaise

1 egg
¼ teaspoon dry mustard
½ teaspoon salt

2 Tablespoons raspberry
  vinegar
1¼-1⅓ cups vegetable oil

In a blender or food processor, combine egg, mustard, salt and vinegar. Add oil at first in droplets, then in a small, steady stream until mayonnaise is desired consistency.

Salad

3 whole chicken breasts; cooked, skinned and cut into ½-inch strips
6 Tablespoons white wine
2 cups fresh peas, cooked
2 cups thinly sliced celery
8 ounces fresh snow peas, cooked tender-crisp

3 medium tomatoes, peeled and cut into 8 wedges
¼ cup minced shallots
¼ cup minced fresh parsley
lettuce leaves
4 hard-cooked eggs, cut into wedges
large green olives
large ripe olives

Marinate chicken in wine for 1 hour. Season to taste.

Combine peas, celery, snow peas, 2 of the tomatoes, shallots and parsley. Fold in enough mayonnaise to moisten.

Arrange lettuce leaves on a large platter. Mound vegetables in the center and arrange chicken around vegetables. Decorate platter with egg wedges, olives and the remaining tomato wedges.

CURRIED CHICKEN SALAD
SERVES: 4

"Nice on a wedge of cantaloupe!"

Dressing

3 ounces cream cheese, softened
¾ cup heavy cream
¼ cup fresh orange juice

1½ teaspoons curry powder
1 teaspoon salt
2 Tablespoons chutney

In a mixing bowl, beat dressing ingredients. Chill.

Salad

2 whole chicken breasts; cooked, skinned and cubed
⅔ cup flaked coconut

2 11-ounce cans Mandarin oranges, drained

To serve, combine salad ingredients with enough dressing to moisten.

CHEYENNE MOUNTAIN CHEF'S SALAD   SERVES: 6

½ cup apple jelly
½ cup vegetable oil
¼ cup fresh lemon juice
½ teaspoon garlic salt
6 cups torn mixed salad greens
4 hard-cooked eggs, sliced
1 cup grated mild Cheddar
   cheese

6 ounces cooked turkey, chicken
   or roast beef, cut into julienne
   strips
½ cup garbanzo beans
1 cup alfalfa sprouts
2 Tablespoons sesame seeds,
   toasted

In a blender or food processor, combine jelly, oil, lemon juice and garlic salt. Chill.

In a large salad bowl, combine remaining ingredients with dressing; toss lightly.

FRUITED CHICKEN SALAD   SERVES: 8
"For a bridge luncheon!"

2½ cups cooked, cubed chicken
1 Tablespoon vegetable oil
1 Tablespoon orange juice
1 Tablespoon white vinegar
½ teaspoon salt
1½ cups cooked rice
¾ cup seedless green grapes

¾ cup sliced celery
1 8-ounce can pineapple chunks,
   drained
1 8-ounce can Mandarin
   oranges, drained
½ cup toasted slivered almonds
½ cup mayonnaise

In a large bowl, combine chicken, oil, orange juice, vinegar and salt. Marinate for 30 minutes. Add remaining ingredients; toss gently. Chill.

BACON SALAD   SERVES: 4

4 strips bacon, sliced
1 egg, beaten
3 Tablespoons sugar
2 Tablespoons water
2 Tablespoons cider vinegar

pinch dry mustard
dash pepper
dash onion salt
fresh lettuce and spinach

Cook and drain bacon; discard grease. Return bacon to skillet. Over low heat, whisk in remaining ingredients except greens. Cook and stir until mixture thickens. Cool. Toss with lettuce and spinach.

BEEF AND AVOCADO SALAD   SERVES: 4
"Superb way to use leftover roast beef!"

3 avocados, pitted and sliced
juice of ½ lemon
1 pound rare roast beef, cut into
   julienne strips
1 small red onion, thinly sliced
½ cup safflower oil
½ cup olive oil

½ cup raspberry or red wine
   vinegar
2 teaspoons Dijon mustard
2 teaspoons salt
¼ teaspoon pepper
1 teaspoon chopped fresh
   parsley
fresh greens

In a bowl, place avocados; toss with lemon juice. Add roast beef and onion rings.

Combine remaining ingredients except greens and pour over salad. Refrigerate several hours, tossing occasionally. Serve in a bowl lined with fresh greens.

PORK 'N' GREENS   SERVES: 6

1 cup sour cream
2 Tablespoons red wine vinegar
2 Tablespoons sugar
1 teaspoon salt

6 cups mixed salad greens
3 green onions, sliced
6 strips bacon, cooked and
crumbled

Combine sour cream, vinegar, sugar and salt. Toss greens with onion and dressing. Sprinkle bacon on top.

SHRIMP MACARONI SALAD   SERVES: 6

1 pound medium shrimp;
   cooked, peeled and de-veined
creamy-style French dressing
2½ cups cooked medium-size
   shell macaroni
1 small onion, minced
1 2-ounce jar stuffed green
   olives, sliced

1 small green pepper, chopped
1½ cups sliced celery
½ cup cider vinegar
½ cup sugar
1 teaspoon dry mustard
4 eggs

Marinate shrimp in French dressing for 2-4 hours. Drain. Combine shrimp with pasta and vegetables.

In the top of a double boiler, combine remaining ingredients. Cook over simmering water until thickened. Season to taste. Fold into salad and chill.

NOTE: Dressing may be made in advance.

SHRIMP-STUFFED ARTICHOKES

SERVES: 6

"A luncheon winner!"

6 artichokes
2 lemons, sliced
3 cups homemade mayonnaise
  (see page 45)
1 Tablespoon tarragon wine
  vinegar
1 teaspoon fresh lemon juice
1 Tablespoon anchovy paste
1 teaspoon tarragon

¼ cup finely chopped green
  onions
¼ teaspoon finely chopped
  garlic
¼ cup finely chopped fresh
  parsley
⅛ teaspoon cayenne pepper
2 pounds large shrimp; cooked,
  peeled and de-veined

Prepare artichokes by breaking off stems, cutting 1 inch off tops and snipping off leaf points with scissors. Rub cut surfaces with lemon.

In a large kettle, bring 6 quarts of salted water to a boil; add artichokes. Boil covered for 40 minutes or until a leaf pulls out easily. Drain upside down. Spread leaves apart, pull out soft center leaves and scoop out choke with a spoon. Chill.

In a blender or food processor, combine all remaining ingredients except shrimp. Adjust seasonings. Reserve 6 shrimp for garnish. Cut remaining shrimp into bite-size pieces. Gently combine shrimp with enough dressing to moisten. Fill artichokes with shrimp mixture. Chill.

Serve artichokes on chilled plates, hooking one whole shrimp over edge of artichoke. Garnish plate with lemon slices. Pass remaining dressing for dipping artichoke leaves.

SHRIMP AND SNOW PEA SALAD

SERVES: 4

Dressing

½ teaspoon salt
¼ teaspoon celery seed
¼ teaspoon sugar
¼ cup vegetable oil

1½ Tablespoons cider vinegar
1 Tablespoon soy sauce
1 teaspoon curry powder

Salad

1½ cups cooked rice
8 ounces fresh snow peas,
  steamed tender-crisp
8 ounces large shrimp; cooked,
  shelled and de-veined

2 Tablespoons chopped green
  onions
¾ cup sliced celery
½ cup cashews

In a large bowl, combine dressing ingredients. Stir in salad ingredients. Chill.

BROADMOOR GINGER DRESSING

YIELD: 3 cups

"Serve over fruit or seafood!"

5 egg yolks
1 teaspoon Dijon mustard
½ teaspoon Worcestershire
   sauce
2 Tablespoons fresh lemon juice
½ teaspoon salt
1½ cups vegetable oil
4 pieces preserved stem ginger

2 Tablespoons honey
1 teaspoon curry powder
2 teaspoons juice from stem
   ginger jar
1 Tablespoon brandy
1 cup heavy cream

In a blender or food processor, thoroughly combine egg yolks, mustard, Worcestershire, lemon juice and salt. Add oil gradually. Add stem ginger, honey, curry powder, ginger juice, brandy and 3 tablespoons of the cream. Blend thoroughly and adjust seasonings.

Whip remaining cream until stiff peaks are formed. Fold into dressing and chill.

CREAMY HONEY DRESSING

YIELD: 2¼ cups

"Great on salad greens!"

1¼ cups mayonnaise
½ cup vegetable oil
¼ cup honey
¼ cup prepared spicy mustard
3 Tablespoons fresh lemon juice
2 green onions, sliced

1 Tablespoon freshly chopped
   parsley
1 teaspoon celery seed
¼ teaspoon dry mustard
¼ teaspoon curry powder

In a blender or food processor, combine all ingredients. Chill.

CREAMY GARLIC SALAD DRESSING

YIELD: 3½ cups

"Excellent for a spinach salad!"

2 cups mayonnaise
1 cup sour cream
½ cup buttermilk
1 teaspoon garlic salt

½ teaspoon garlic powder
½ teaspoon onion powder
1 Tablespoon dried parsley
1 teaspoon dried chives

Blend all ingredients and chill.

ORANGE VINAIGRETTE
SALAD DRESSING

YIELD: 1½ cups

½ cup orange juice
1 cup vegetable oil
¼ cup sugar
3 Tablespoons red wine vinegar

½ teaspoon salt
1 teaspoon grated fresh orange
  peel

In a jar, combine all ingredients and shake well. Chill.

NOTE: Delicious over a salad of mixed greens, avocado, Mandarin oranges and green onions.

MAYONNAISE

YIELD: 1½ cups

1 egg
1 Tablespoon fresh lemon juice
  or white wine vinegar
1 Tablespoon Dijon mustard

½ teaspoon salt
pinch cayenne pepper
1¼ cups vegetable oil

In a food processor or blender, combine egg, lemon juice, mustard, salt and cayenne. With machine running, slowly add oil in a small stream. Refrigerate.

BELVEDERE SALAD DRESSING

YIELD: 2 cups

1½ cups safflower oil
½ cup red wine vinegar
15 black peppercorns
1½ teaspoons sweet basil
1½ teaspoons garlic salt

1 bay leaf
dash Tabasco sauce
1½ Tablespoons Worcestershire
  sauce

In a blender or food processor, combine all ingredients thoroughly. Chill. Best prepared several days in advance.

To make cleanup easier, oil the measuring cup before measuring quantities of honey, syrup or molasses.

FRUIT SALAD DRESSING

YIELD: 1¼ cups

⅓ cup honey
2 Tablespoons cider vinegar
1 Tablespoon frozen orange
  juice concentrate

1 Tablespoon prepared mustard
1 teaspoon salt
¾ cup vegetable oil
1 Tablespoon poppy seeds

Combine honey, vinegar, orange juice, mustard and salt. Add oil slowly, beating well. Stir in poppy seeds. Chill.

CRÈME FRAICHE

YIELD: 2 cups

"Use as you would heavy cream!"

2 cups heavy cream

3 Tablespoons buttermilk

In a jar, combine cream and buttermilk; shake well. Allow to stand in a warm place for 24 hours. When mixture has thickened, refrigerate for at least 24 hours before using. Keeps well for 2-4 weeks. May be whipped.

CELERY SEED DRESSING

YIELD: 1½ cups

"Especially good on fruit!"

⅔ cup sugar
2 Tablespoons chopped onion
1 teaspoon salt
1 teaspoon celery seed

1 Tablespoon prepared mustard
⅓ cup cider vinegar
1 cup vegetable oil

In a blender or food processor, combine all ingredients. Chill.

MINT DRESSING

YIELD: 1½ cups

"Dare to dress fruit in this!"

½ cup sugar
2½ Tablespoons cornstarch
1 cup pineapple juice

3 Tablespoons crushed fresh
  mint leaves
juice of 1 medium lemon
juice of 1 medium orange

In a saucepan, combine sugar and cornstarch. Whisk in pineapple juice; cook until clear. Remove from heat and stir in mint. Cool. Add the fruit juices; strain. Refrigerate for up to 10 days.

BREADS

CRIPPLE CREEK was a real gold boom town! In 1881, after the discovery of gold, it changed from a serene little pasture on the back side of Pikes Peak to a frantic, bustling city where an estimated 50,000 people rushed to get rich. Instant wealth could be had by laboring under the ground for buried gold or by fleecing miners who had already struck it rich! Giant fortunes were made every day on the end of a pick or the turn of a card. The town bristled with saloons and fancy houses, and the whistles of incoming and outgoing trains split the air day and night. Several daily papers grew and thrived in what must have been a publisher's dream. Bankers attained prominence in a single season! More gold came out of the Cripple Creek area during its peak than from any other gold field in the world. All told, more than $700,000,000 in Cripple Creek gold found its way into the American economy. However, the prospectors of the boom years were frustrated because they believed that the "Golden Bowl"—Cripple Creek's mother lode—was never tapped. If they were right, all that gold is still waiting to be discovered!

BREADS

*Found elsewhere in the book.

STRAWBERRY BREAD

YIELD: 2 loaves

"Perfect for luncheons!"

3 cups flour
1 teaspoon baking soda
1 teaspoon cinnamon
2 cups sugar
1 teaspoon salt
1¼ cups vegetable oil
4 eggs

2 10-ounce packages frozen
   strawberries, thawed
   (reserve ½ cup juice and a few
   berries for filling)
1 8-ounce package cream
   cheese, softened

In a mixing bowl, combine flour, soda, cinnamon, sugar and salt. Add oil, eggs and strawberries; mix well. Pour into two greased 9-inch loaf pans. Bake at 350° for 50-60 minutes. Allow to cool for 10 minutes before removing from pan.

Beat cream cheese with reserved strawberries and juice to make a spreading consistency. Cut bread into thin slices. To make sandwiches, spread 1 slice with cream cheese filling. Top with a second slice; cut in half to serve.

NOTE: Bread slices best when frozen.

RHUBARB BREAD

YIELD: 2 loaves

1½ cups brown sugar
⅔ cup vegetable oil
1 egg
1 cup buttermilk
1 teaspoon baking soda
1½ teaspoons cinnamon
1 teaspoon salt

1 teaspoon vanilla
2½ cups flour
2 cups ¼-inch pieces rhubarb
½ cup chopped pecans
⅓ cup sugar
1 Tablespoon butter, melted

In a large bowl, beat brown sugar, oil and egg.

In another bowl, combine buttermilk, soda, cinnamon, salt and vanilla. Add milk mixture to sugar mixture alternately with flour; beat well after each addition.

Fold in rhubarb and pecans. Turn into two greased and floured 8-inch loaf pans. Mix sugar with butter; sprinkle on loaves. Bake at 350° for 35-45 minutes.

BANANA BREAD

YIELD: 1 loaf

"For a morning meeting!"

½ cup butter, softened
1 cup sugar
2 eggs
3 ripe bananas, mashed
2 cups flour

1 teaspoon salt
1 teaspoon baking soda mixed
   with 3 Tablespoons cold water
1 teaspoon vanilla
½ cup chopped pecans
   or walnuts

In a mixing bowl, cream butter and sugar. Add eggs and bananas. Beat
in remaining ingredients. Pour into a greased 9-inch loaf pan. Bake at 350°
for 40-45 minutes.

APRICOT NUT BREAD

YIELD: 1 loaf

¾ cup dried apricots
1 egg
2 Tablespoons butter, melted
1 cup sugar
1 Tablespoon baking powder

¼ teaspoon baking soda
½ teaspoon salt
2 cups flour
¾ cup orange juice
¾ cup chopped pecans

Cook apricots in boiling water for 4 minutes; drain and cut into quarters.

In a mixing bowl, beat egg, butter, sugar, baking powder, soda and salt.
Stir in flour alternately with orange juice. Add apricots and nuts. Pour
into a greased and floured 8-inch loaf pan. Bake at 350° for 40-45 minutes.

BEER BREAD

YIELD: 1 loaf

3 cups self-rising flour
2 Tablespoons sugar

1 12-ounce can beer,
   room temperature

In a mixing bowl, combine flour and sugar. Add beer; mix. Batter will
be slightly lumpy. Pour into a greased 8-inch loaf pan; spread evenly.
Let bread stand at room temperature for 10 minutes. Bake at 375° for
30-35 minutes.

NOTE: For a lighter batter, use 3 cups Bisquick instead of flour. Batter
may be poured into well-greased muffin tins. Bake at 450° for 15-18
minutes. YIELD: 18 muffins.

PUMPKIN BREAD (½ this recipe)
"Fun, Fall flavor!"

YIELD: 2 loaves

3½ cups flour
1 teaspoon baking powder
1 teaspoon salt
1 teaspoon cinnamon
1 teaspoon baking soda
1 teaspoon nutmeg

3 cups sugar
1 cup vegetable oil
4 eggs
1 16-ounce can pumpkin
⅔ cup water

Combine flour, baking powder, salt, cinnamon, soda and nutmeg; set aside.

In a bowl, thoroughly combine sugar, oil, eggs and pumpkin. To pumpkin mixture, add water alternately with dry ingredients. Pour batter into two 9-inch or four 7-inch greased loaf pans. Bake at 350° for 45-55 minutes. Check small pans at 30 minutes.

CITRUS ZUCCHINI BREAD

YIELD: 1 loaf

1 cup sugar
½ cup vegetable oil
2 eggs
1 teaspoon lemon extract
½ teaspoon orange extract
1½ cups flour
2 teaspoons baking powder

½ teaspoon baking soda
½ teaspoon salt
⅛ teaspoon nutmeg
½ teaspoon ginger
1½ cups grated zucchini
½ cup chopped pecans
   or walnuts

In a mixing bowl, beat sugar, oil, eggs and extracts. Add all dry ingredients; mix well. Stir in zucchini and nuts. Pour into greased 9-inch loaf pan. Bake at 375° for 45-55 minutes. Cool in pan for 10 minutes before removing.

SUNSHINE BREAD

YIELD: 2 loaves

1 3-ounce package lemon
   gelatin
1 cup water
4 eggs

¾ cup vegetable oil
1 18½-ounce package
   white cake mix

Dissolve gelatin in hot water and cool.

Stir gelatin, eggs and oil into cake mix. Beat for 4 minutes. Pour into two greased and floured 8½-inch loaf pans. Bake at 350° for 35-40 minutes. Allow to cool 10 minutes before removing from pan.

ZUCCHINI BREAD

YIELD: 2 loaves

3 cups flour
1 teaspoon salt
1 teaspoon baking soda
½ teaspoon baking powder
1 teaspoon cinnamon
½ teaspoon nutmeg
3 eggs
1 cup brown sugar

1 cup sugar
1 cup vegetable oil
1 teaspoon vanilla
2 cups grated zucchini
1 cup chopped walnuts
  or pecans
1 cup raisins
1 8-ounce can crushed pineapple

In a large bowl, mix flour, salt, soda, baking powder, cinnamon and nutmeg. Add eggs, sugars, oil and vanilla. Mix thoroughly. Fold in zucchini, nuts, raisins and pineapple. Pour batter into greased and floured loaf pans. For two large loaves (9-inch), bake at 350° for 50-60 minutes. For four small loaves (7-inch), bake at 350° for 35-45 minutes.

LEMON BREAD

YIELD: 1 loaf

1½ cups sugar
6 Tablespoons margarine
3 eggs
1 Tablespoon lemon extract
grated peel of 1 medium lemon

½ cup milk
1½ cups flour
1½ teaspoons baking powder
¼ teaspoon salt
3 Tablespoons fresh lemon juice

Cream 1 cup sugar and margarine. Add eggs, extract, lemon peel and milk. Beat in flour, baking powder and salt. Pour into greased and floured 9-inch loaf pan. Bake at 350° for 30-40 minutes.

Combine lemon juice and ½ cup sugar. Remove bread from oven and top with mixture. Return to oven for 10 minutes. Cool for 30 minutes; remove from pan.

DATE MUFFINS

YIELD: 18

1 teaspoon baking soda
1 cup hot water
1 cup chopped dates
½ cup shortening

1 cup sugar
1½ cups flour
2 eggs, beaten
1 teaspoon salt

Dissolve soda in hot water; add dates. Let soak until cool.

Combine remaining ingredients. Stir in dates. Fill greased muffin tins two-thirds full. Bake at 350° for 15-20 minutes.

BLUEBERRY BOY BAIT

YIELD: 2 dozen

2 cups flour
1½ cups sugar
¾ cup shortening
2 teaspoons baking powder
2 eggs, room temperature
 and separated

1 teaspoon salt
1 cup milk
1 teaspoon vanilla
1 pint fresh blueberries,
 washed and stemmed

Blend flour, sugar and shortening. Reserve ¾ cup for topping. To remaining flour mixture, add baking powder, egg yolks, salt, milk and vanilla.

Beat egg whites until stiff; fold into batter. Pour into greased and floured 9 x 13-inch pan. Sprinkle with blueberries and reserved topping. Bake at 350° for 35-45 minutes.

OLD-FASHIONED OAT MUFFINS

YIELD: 18

1 cup old-fashioned oats
1 cup buttermilk
1 cup flour
1 teaspoon baking powder
½ teaspoon baking soda
½ teaspoon salt

1 cup brown sugar
1 egg, beaten
¼ cup butter, melted
½ cup raisins
grated peel of 1 orange

In a bowl, place oats and buttermilk; let stand for 10 minutes.

Combine flour, baking powder, soda, salt and sugar. Add egg and butter; mix well. Stir in buttermilk mixture, raisins and orange peel. Fill greased muffin tins two-thirds full. Bake at 400° for 20 minutes.

APPLESAUCE MUFFINS

YIELD: 16

½ cup butter, softened
1 cup sugar
1 egg
1 cup applesauce
2 cups flour

1 teaspoon baking soda
¼ teaspoon salt
1 teaspoon ground allspice
1 teaspoon cinnamon
¼ teaspoon ground cloves

Cream butter and sugar. Add egg and applesauce. Stir in remaining ingredients. Fill greased muffin tins two-thirds full. Bake at 400° for 15-20 minutes.

NOTE: Batter may be refrigerated for up to 6 weeks.

BRAN MUFFINS

YIELD: 2½ dozen

1 cup boiling water
1 cup All-Bran cereal
1½ cups sugar
½ cup margarine
2 eggs

2 cups Bran Buds cereal
2 cups buttermilk
2 teaspoons baking soda
½ teaspoon salt
2½ cups flour

Pour boiling water over the All-Bran; set aside.

Cream sugar and margarine. Beat in eggs, All-Bran mixture and remaining ingredients. Fill greased muffin tins two-thirds full. Bake at 375° for 15-20 minutes.

NOTE: Unused batter may be kept in an airtight container in refrigerator for 6 weeks.

ORANGE MUFFINS

YIELD: 4 dozen miniature muffins

1 cup butter, softened
1 cup sugar
2 eggs
1 teaspoon baking soda
1 cup buttermilk
2 cups sifted flour

grated peel of 2 oranges
½ cup chopped pecans
  or golden raisins
juice of 2 oranges
1 cup brown sugar

Cream butter and sugar; add eggs. Dissolve soda in buttermilk. Add to sugar mixture alternately with flour. Stir in orange peel and nuts. Fill greased miniature muffin tins one-half full. Bake at 375° for 12-15 minutes. Combine orange juice and brown sugar; set aside.

After baking, remove muffins from oven; drizzle orange juice mixture over muffins. Remove from pans immediately.

WHOLE WHEAT WAFFLES

YIELD: 4 8-inch waffles

"Serve with Escalloped Bacon!"

2 cups whole wheat flour
1 Tablespoon brown sugar
1 teaspoon baking powder
¼ teaspoon salt

2 eggs
1½ cups milk
¼ cup butter, melted

Combine flour, sugar, baking powder and salt. Add eggs, milk and butter, beating until batter is smooth. Pour batter onto hot waffle iron. Bake until brown.

APPLE PANCAKE

SERVES: 4

"A breakfast change of pace!"

Pancake

3 Tablespoons butter
2 apples; peeled, cored and
   thinly sliced
3 eggs

½ cup milk
1 teaspoon sugar
½ cup flour

In a 10-inch oven-proof skillet, melt butter. Add apples; saute until
soft. Whisk together eggs, milk, sugar, flour and dash of salt. Pour over
apples. Bake at 400° for 10 minutes.

Topping

¼ cup sugar
1 teaspoon cinnamon

2 Tablespoons butter
maple syrup

Combine sugar and cinnamon. Remove skillet from oven. Sprinkle
sugar-cinnamon topping on baked pancake and dot with butter. Return
to oven for 2 minutes. Serve immediately with maple syrup.

YOGURT PANCAKES

SERVES: 4

1 egg
1 8-ounce carton flavored
   yogurt
¾ cup milk
2 Tablespoons vegetable oil
1 cup flour

1 Tablespoon sugar
2 teaspoons baking powder
½ teaspoon salt
½ teaspoon baking soda
warmed syrup

In a medium bowl, beat the egg with a fork until frothy. Add yogurt, milk
and oil. Beat until well blended; set aside.

In a large bowl, combine dry ingredients. Add egg mixture and stir only
until blended. Batter will be lumpy and thick. Cook on oiled griddle.
Serve immediately with butter and syrup.

To proof yeast: combine yeast, a small quantity of sugar and liquid at 105°
to 115° Allow to stand for 2-3 minutes. If yeast mixture bubbles, it is
active and will leaven recipe.

ORANGE CRESCENT ROLLS
YIELD: 2 dozen

"These disappear fast!"

Orange Rolls

1 package dry yeast	½ cup sour cream
¼ cup water (105°-115°)	10 Tablespoons butter, melted
1 cup sugar	2½ to 3 cups flour
1 teaspoon salt	grated peel of 3 medium oranges
2 eggs	

Dissolve yeast in warm water with 1 teaspoon sugar. Let stand for 2-3 minutes.

In a bowl, combine ¼ cup sugar, salt, eggs, sour cream, 6 tablespoons melted butter and the yeast mixture. Gradually add 2 cups flour. Beat until smooth. Knead in enough remaining flour to make a soft dough. Let rise until doubled.

Combine ¾ cup sugar and orange peel. Set aside.

Divide dough into 2 parts. Roll half of the dough into a 9-inch circle. Brush dough with 2 tablespoons butter and sprinkle with half of the orange-sugar mixture. Cut into 12 wedges. Roll up, starting with wide end. Place point-side down on greased baking sheet. Repeat with remaining dough. Cover and let rise until almost doubled. Bake at 350° for 18 minutes or until lightly browned. Top rolls with glaze while still warm.

Orange Glaze

¾ cup sugar	1 Tablespoon orange juice
½ cup sour cream	concentrate
	¼ cup butter

In a saucepan, combine glaze ingredients. Boil for 3 minutes, stirring constantly. Spoon over warm rolls.

BAKED CHEESE PANCAKES
YIELD: 1½ dozen

8 ounces Farmer's cheese, grated	¼ cup sugar
	½ teaspoon vanilla
1 3-ounce package cream cheese, softened	½ cup wheat germ
	berries or syrup
1 egg	

Mix Farmer's cheese, cream cheese, egg, sugar and vanilla. Form mixture into small balls; roll in wheat germ.

Place on greased baking sheet and bake at 375° for 20 minutes or until golden brown. Serve with berries or syrup.

MAPLE NUT TWISTS

YIELD: 2 coffeecakes

"Presentation is spectacular!"

Dough

2 packages dry yeast
½ cup water (105°-115°)
1 teaspoon maple flavoring
1¾ cups milk, warmed
½ cup butter, melted

½ cup sugar
1½ teaspoons salt
2 eggs
7 cups flour

Dissolve yeast in warm water with 1 teaspoon sugar. Set aside for 2-3 minutes.

In a mixing bowl, combine yeast mixture, maple flavoring, warm milk, butter, ½ cup sugar, salt and eggs. Beat in 5 cups flour. Add enough additional flour to make a soft dough. Knead for 8 minutes. Place dough in greased bowl; turn once to grease top. Cover and let rise until doubled.

Filling

1⅓ cups sugar
4 teaspoons cinnamon

2 teaspoons maple flavoring
1 cup chopped pecans

Combine all filling ingredients. Set aside.

¾ cup butter, melted

Divide dough into 6 equal portions to make 2 coffeecakes. For each coffeecake, use 3 portions of dough. Roll 1 portion to a 14-inch diameter. Place on a pizza pan and brush with 2 tablespoons melted butter; sprinkle with a scant ½ cup of filling. Continue in the same manner with other 2 portions of dough to make 3 layers.

Place a drinking glass in the center of the pizza pan on top of the dough layers. Using a sharp knife, cut through all 3 layers of dough beginning at the glass and cutting to the edge of the circle. Cut 16 equal wedges. Twist each wedge three times. Remove glass. Cover coffeecake and let rise until almost doubled. Repeat entire process for second coffeecake. Bake at 375° for 20 minutes or until golden. Glaze coffeecakes while warm.

Glaze

3 cups powdered sugar
1 teaspoon maple flavoring
milk

Combine powdered sugar, maple flavoring and enough milk to make a glaze consistency. Drizzle over coffeecakes.

NOTE: Freezes very well.

SOURDOUGH FRENCH BREAD
YIELD: 2 loaves

"Prospectors made this!"

1 package dry yeast
1 ½ Tablespoons sugar
¼ cup warm water
  (105°-115°)
½ cup milk
1 cup water
1 ½ Tablespoons vegetable oil

4 cups flour
2 ½ teaspoons salt
2 Tablespoons sourdough
  starter, room temperature
1 egg white beaten with
  1 Tablespoon water

Dissolve yeast with sugar in ¼ cup warm water; set aside for 2-3 minutes.

Heat milk, 1 cup water and oil to lukewarm.

In a large bowl, place flour and salt. Make a well in the center. Pour
all liquids into well; add starter and stir until well blended. Do not knead.
Dough will be soft. Cover and let rise in warm place until doubled.

Turn onto lightly floured board. Divide into 2 portions. Roll each portion
into a 10 x 15-inch rectangle. Roll up tightly, beginning at the wide side;
seal edges by pinching together. Place seam-side down in a greased
double baguette pan. With a sharp knife, make diagonal slashes in dough
every 3 inches. Cover and let rise in a warm place until almost doubled.
Bake at 425° for 15 minutes. Reduce heat to 350°; bake for 10
minutes. Brush top and sides with egg white mixture. Bake for 5 minutes.

SOURDOUGH STARTER
YIELD: 2 cups

1 package dry yeast
2 teaspoons sugar
¾ cup water (105°-115°)
¼ cup milk

2 teaspoons vegetable oil
1 ½ teaspoons salt
2 ⅓ cups flour

Dissolve yeast and sugar in warm water. Stir in remaining ingredients,
mixing just enough to blend thoroughly. Cover; let stand in a warm place
for 12-18 hours to sour. This is enough starter for 12 loaves.

NOTE: Remaining starter may be stored covered in refrigerator for several
days or divided into portions and frozen. Measure amount needed for bread;
bring to room temperature before adding to bread mixture.

SQUAW BREAD
"A fine texture!"

YIELD: 2 loaves

1¾ cups water
½ cup corn meal
2 teaspoons salt
½ cup light molasses
2 Tablespoons butter

1 package dry yeast
1 teaspoon sugar
½ cup water (105°-115°)
5 cups flour

In a saucepan, combine water, corn meal and salt. Cook until thick; remove from heat. Stir in molasses and butter.

Dissolve yeast and sugar in warm water; set aside for 2-3 minutes. In a mixing bowl, place corn meal mixture and 2 cups flour; beat well. Add yeast mixture and enough flour to make a soft dough. Knead for 8-10 minutes. Place in greased bowl, turning to grease top. Cover and let rise until doubled.

Divide dough in half. On a surface sprinkled with corn meal, shape each half into a round loaf. Place in greased 8-inch round pans; cover and let rise until almost doubled. Bake at 375° for 30 minutes.

SWEDISH RYE BREAD
"Excellent with corned beef!"

YIELD: 2 loaves

1 package dry yeast
2½ cups rye flour
¼ cup brown sugar
¼ cup dark corn syrup
1 Tablespoon salt

2 Tablespoons shortening
1¾ cups water
3 Tablespoons caraway seeds
3 cups flour

In a large mixing bowl, combine yeast and rye flour.

In a saucepan, simmer brown sugar, corn syrup, salt, shortening and water. Slowly add to yeast mixture; beat for 2 minutes. Add caraway seeds and enough white flour to make a soft dough. Knead for 8 minutes.

Place dough in lightly greased bowl; turn once to grease top. Cover and let rise until doubled, approximately 2 hours.

Punch down. Divide dough in half and place in two 8-inch greased loaf pans. Cover and let rise until almost doubled, approximately 1½ hours. Bake at 375° for 30 minutes.

NOTE: Dough may be formed into 2 round loaves and placed on opposite corners of a greased baking sheet. Bake as directed.

DUTCH BREAD

YIELD: 3 loaves

"Almost a coffeecake!"

Bread

1 package dry yeast	¼ teaspoon salt
½ cup water (105°-115°)	¾ cup hot milk
¾ cup cooked, mashed potatoes	2 eggs, beaten
½ cup margarine	4-4½ cups flour
¾ cup sugar	

Dissolve yeast and 1 teaspoon sugar in warm water. Set aside for 2-3 minutes.

In a large mixing bowl, place mashed potatoes, margarine, sugar, salt and hot milk. Stir until dissolved. Add eggs and yeast mixture. Beat in 2 cups flour. Add additional flour to make a soft dough. Knead for 8 minutes. Place in a greased bowl; grease top of dough. Cover and let rise until doubled.

Punch down. Divide dough into 3 equal portions; roll each piece into a 9-inch circle. Place each circle into a greased 9-inch round cake pan. Cover and let rise until almost doubled. Prepare topping.

Topping

1½ cups flour	1 teaspoon salt
¾ cup brown sugar	½ cup butter, softened

Blend topping ingredients to make crumbs. Brush top of each risen loaf with warm water; cover each with topping. Bake at 350° for 30-40 minutes.

MOLASSES WHEAT BREAD

YIELD: 2 loaves

2 cups water (120°-130°)	1 Tablespoon salt
3 Tablespoons shortening	2½ cups whole wheat flour
¼ cup light molasses	2 packages dry yeast
½ cup nonfat dry milk	2½ cups flour

In a mixing bowl, combine water, shortening, molasses, milk, salt and 1 cup whole wheat flour; add yeast. Beat for 1 minute. Add remaining whole wheat flour; beat for 3 minutes. Work in enough white flour to make a soft dough; knead for 6 minutes. Place in a greased bowl, turning to grease top. Cover and let rise until doubled.

Punch down; knead for 30 seconds. Divide dough in half. Place in two greased 8-inch loaf pans. Cover and let rise until almost doubled. Bake at 375° for 30-35 minutes.

SUPER REFRIGERATOR ROLLS

YIELD: 4 dozen

1 package dry yeast
¼ cup water (105°-115°)
½ cup sugar
¼ cup butter
2 cups milk, warmed

1 egg
6-7 cups flour
1 teaspoon salt
½ teaspoon baking soda
1 teaspoon baking powder

Dissolve yeast in warm water with 1 teaspoon sugar. Set aside for
2-3 minutes.

In a large bowl, dissolve ½ cup sugar and butter in warm milk. Beat in
yeast mixture and egg. Beat in 2 cups flour, salt, soda and baking powder.
Add additional flour to make a soft dough; knead for 8 minutes. Store
in a large, greased and covered container; grease top of dough. Refrigerate
12-24 hours. Dough will keep in refrigerator for 1 week if punched
down daily.

NOTE: To make crescent rolls, divide dough into fourths; roll each quarter
into a 12-inch circle. Cut into 12 wedges; roll up each wedge starting
with wide end. Place point down forming into a crescent shape on a greased
baking sheet. Cover and let rise until almost doubled. Bake at 400° for
10-15 minutes.

ONION BRAID BREAD

YIELD: 3 loaves

2 packages dry yeast
1 envelope dry onion soup mix
⅓ cup sugar
2 Tablespoons light molasses
1 teaspoon salt

1 egg
⅓ cup shortening
6½ cups flour
2 cups water (120°-130°)

In a mixing bowl, combine yeast, soup mix, sugar, molasses, salt, egg,
shortening and 2 cups flour. Add hot water and beat for 1 minute. Mix
in additional flour to make a soft dough; knead 8-10 minutes. Place
in a greased bowl. Grease surface of dough; cover and let rise until doubled.

Punch down and divide dough into 9 equal parts. By hand, roll each portion
into a 14-inch strand. On a baking sheet, braid 3 strands to make a loaf;
tuck ends under. Repeat for 2 remaining loaves. Cover with greased plastic
wrap and let rise until almost doubled. Bake at 375° for 25-30 minutes.

SOUR CREAM DINNER ROLLS

YIELD: 2 dozen

1 package dry yeast
½ cup water (105°-115°)
1 cup sour cream, warmed
3 Tablespoons sugar
2 Tablespoons butter, melted

1 teaspoon salt
1 egg
⅛ teaspoon baking soda
3½ cups flour

Dissolve yeast in warm water with 1 teaspoon sugar; set aside for 2-3 minutes.

In a mixing bowl, combine sour cream, sugar, butter, salt and egg. Beat in yeast mixture, soda and 1 cup flour. Add remaining flour to make a soft dough. Knead for 8 minutes. Cover and let rest for 20 minutes.

Shape into 24 balls. Divide balls evenly between two greased 9-inch round baking pans. Cover and let rise until almost doubled. Bake at 375° for 20 minutes.

WHEAT BERRY BATTER BREAD

YIELD: 1 loaf

"A crunchy texture!"

Wheat Berries
½ cup wheat berries

In a large saucepan, combine wheat berries and 1 quart water. Cover and let stand for 8 hours or boil 2 minutes and let stand for 1 hour. Without draining berries, bring to a boil over high heat. Reduce heat and simmer until tender, about 2 hours. Drain and cool. Makes approximately 1½ cups. Cooked berries may be frozen.

Bread
2¼ cups flour
1 Tablespoon sugar
1 teaspoon salt
1 package dry yeast

1 cup water (120°-130°)
½ cup cooked wheat berries
corn meal
1 Tablespoon butter, melted

In a mixing bowl, combine 1½ cups flour, sugar, salt and yeast. Add hot liquid. Beat for 3 minutes. Add wheat berries and remaining ¾ cup flour. Dough should be very elastic and soft. Cover and let rise until doubled. Stir dough down. Grease 8-inch loaf pan; coat with corn meal. Spoon dough into pan; let rise until almost doubled. Bake at 375° for 30 minutes. Brush top with melted butter.

HONEY-OAT WHEAT BREAD   YIELD: 2 loaves

2½ cups buttermilk   2 packages dry yeast
½ cup honey   1 Tablespoon salt
⅓ cup butter   2 eggs
3½ cups flour   2½-3 cups whole wheat flour
1½ cups old-fashioned oats

In a saucepan, heat buttermilk, honey and butter until 120°-130°.

In a large mixing bowl, place white flour, oats, yeast, salt, eggs and buttermilk mixture. Beat for 3 minutes at medium speed. Stir in enough whole wheat flour to make a soft dough; knead for 8 minutes. Place dough in greased bowl; grease top of dough. Cover; let rise until doubled.

Divide dough in half. Place in two greased 9-inch loaf pans. Brush with melted butter. Cover and let rise until almost doubled. Bake at 350° for 25-30 minutes.

THREE-FLOUR BREAD   YIELD: 2 loaves
"A family favorite!"

2 packages dry yeast   ½ cup brown sugar
3½ cups white flour   3 Tablespoons shortening
1½ cups whole wheat flour   2 Tablespoons sugar
½ cup rye flour   2 teaspoons salt
2 cups milk

In a bowl, combine yeast, 1 cup white flour, 1½ cups whole wheat flour and ½ cup rye flour.

In a saucepan, heat milk, brown sugar, shortening, sugar and salt; stir until fat is melted and mixture is warm. Add warm liquid to flour mixture. Beat for 3 minutes.

Add additional 2½ cups white flour or enough to make a soft dough; knead for 8 minutes. Place dough in greased bowl; grease surface of dough. Cover and let rise until doubled, approximately 1½ hours.

Punch dough down, shape into 2 loaves and place in greased 8-inch loaf pans. Let rise until almost doubled. Bake at 375° for 30 minutes.

CINNAMON SWIRL BREAD

YIELD: 2 loaves

"For breakfast!"

1 package dry yeast	5-5½ cups flour
⅓ cup warm water	2 eggs
(105°-115°)	1½ cups old-fashioned oats
1½ cups warm milk	⅓ cup sugar
½ cup sugar	2 teaspoons cinnamon
2 teaspoons salt	3 Tablespoons butter, melted
⅓ cup shortening	

Dissolve yeast in warm water with 1 teaspoon sugar. Set aside for 2-3 minutes.

In a mixing bowl, combine milk, ½ cup sugar, salt and shortening; stir until shortening melts. Add 1 cup flour, eggs, yeast mixture and oats. Beat for 2 minutes. Stir in additional flour to make a soft dough; knead for 8 minutes. Place dough in greased bowl; turn to grease top. Cover and let rise until doubled.

Punch down dough and let rest for 5 minutes. In a small bowl, combine ⅓ cup sugar and cinnamon. Divide dough in half. Roll each half into an 8 x 15-inch rectangle. Brush with 1½ tablespoons butter; sprinkle with half of the cinnamon-sugar mixture. Roll up, jellyroll fashion, starting at short end. Repeat with second loaf. Place in greased 9-inch loaf pans; cover and let rise until almost doubled. Bake at 375° for 30-35 minutes.

ENGLISH MUFFIN LOAF

YIELD: 1 loaf

"Toasts beautifully!"

3 cups flour	⅛ teaspoon baking soda
1 package dry yeast	1 cup milk, warmed
1½ teaspoons sugar	¼ cup water
1 teaspoon salt	corn meal

In a food processor fitted with a steel blade, combine 1½ cups flour, yeast, sugar, salt and soda; process to mix.

Heat liquids until hot (120°-130°). With food processor running, add liquids to dry mixture. Add remaining 1½ cups flour; process for 1 minute.

Place dough into an 8-inch bread pan that has been greased and sprinkled with corn meal. Sprinkle top of dough with corn meal. Cover; allow to rise in a warm place approximately 45 minutes. Bake at 400° for 25 minutes.

NOTE: Great with Creamy Honey Butter (see page 63).

SWEDISH TEA RING
YIELD: 1 tea ring
"For a holiday treat!"

Tea Ring

1 package dry yeast	3⅓ cups flour
¼ cup water (105°-115°)	¼ cup sugar
1¼ cups heavy cream, warmed	1 teaspoon salt
3 egg yolks	½ cup butter

In a small bowl, dissolve yeast and 1 teaspoon sugar in warm water; set aside for 2-3 minutes. Whisk in cream and egg yolks; set aside.

In a large bowl, combine flour, ¼ cup sugar and salt. Cut in butter with pastry blender until coarse and crumbly. Stir in yeast mixture just to moisten. Cover bowl with plastic wrap and refrigerate overnight.

Filling

1 cup walnuts	½ cup sugar
1 Tablespoon cinnamon	¼ cup butter, melted

Topping

1 egg white, slightly beaten	2 Tablespoons butter
1 cup powdered sugar	¼ cup half-and-half

In a food processor or blender, combine filling ingredients except butter until finely ground.

Turn dough onto floured surface and knead for 30 seconds. Roll into a 20 x 24-inch rectangle. Brush with ¼ cup melted butter and spread walnut filling evenly over surface. Starting at long side, roll up dough jellyroll fashion; seal seam. On a greased baking sheet, form dough into a ring, seam-side down, fitting ends together. With a sharp knife, make diagonal cuts in top of dough about 2 inches apart. Brush with egg white. Cover and let rise in a warm place until almost doubled. Bake at 350° for 30-35 minutes. Cool slightly. Combine remaining topping ingredients. Drizzle over tea ring.

CREAMY HONEY BUTTER
YIELD: ¾ cup
"Great on breads!"

¼ cup butter, softened	⅓ cup honey
4 ounces cream cheese, softened	1 teaspoon grated fresh orange peel (optional)

Cream butter and cream cheese. Beat honey into creamed mixture. If desired, add orange peel. Chill.

NOTE: A whiz to make in the food processor.

CINNAMON ROLLS

YIELD: 1½ dozen

"Like Grandma's!"

Rolls

1 package dry yeast	1 teaspoon salt
¼ cup water (105°-115°)	1 egg
1 cup milk	3-3½ cups flour
2 Tablespoons sugar	¼ cup brown sugar
6 Tablespoons butter	

Dissolve yeast in warm water with 1 teaspoon sugar; set aside for 2-3 minutes. Heat milk. Add 2 tablespoons sugar and 3 tablespoons butter to milk; stir until butter melts. Cool to lukewarm; stir in yeast mixture and salt. Beat egg into yeast mixture.

In a large bowl, place 3 cups flour. Mix in yeast mixture, adding more flour if needed to form a soft dough. Knead dough on a floured surface for 5 minutes. Place dough in a greased bowl, turning to grease surface of dough. Cover and let rise until doubled.

Prepare two 8-inch round baking pans by spreading each with 1½ tablespoons melted butter and 2 tablespoons brown sugar. Set aside.

Filling

3 Tablespoons butter	1½ teaspoons cinnamon
½ cup sugar	

Punch dough down and divide in half. Roll each piece on a floured surface to an 8 x 11-inch rectangle. Brush each with 1½ tablespoons melted butter. Combine sugar and cinnamon; sprinkle half of the sugar-cinnamon mixture on each rectangle. Roll dough jellyroll fashion, starting with 8-inch side. Seal edge with water. Cut the roll into eight 1-inch slices. Place 7 slices around the edge of each pan and 1 slice in the center. Repeat procedure with remaining dough. Cover; let rise until almost doubled. Bake at 375° for 20-25 minutes. Remove from oven, run a knife around the edge of the pan and immediately invert onto serving platter.

NOTE: For pecan rolls, sprinkle pecans in the bottom of the prepared pans.

PITA BREAD CHEESE WEDGES

YIELD: 48 triangles

½ cup butter, softened
6 pita breads

¾ cup grated Parmesan cheese

Split each bread in half and then each piece into quarters. Brush butter on rough side of bread and sprinkle with cheese. Place on baking sheet and broil 5 inches from broiler until lightly toasted.

ALMOND PASTRY
"Unusual!"

YIELD: 2 dozen

Crust

1 cup flour
3 Tablespoons sugar
¼ teaspoon salt

½ cup margarine, softened
2 Tablespoons water

In a bowl, stir flour, sugar and salt. Cut in margarine. Add water and mix until pastry holds together. With lightly floured hands, press pastry into bottom of 9 x 13-inch pan.

Filling

1 cup water
½ cup butter

1 cup sifted flour
4 eggs

In a saucepan, heat water and butter until melted. Remove from heat and add flour all at once. Beat vigorously until mixture becomes a thick paste. Return to heat and cook for 1 minute. Off heat, add eggs one at a time, mixing well after each addition. Spread the paste over pastry base. Bake at 400° for 35 minutes. Pastry will puff but deflate as it cools.

Frosting

1 Tablespoon butter, softened
2 cups powdered sugar
5 Tablespoons milk

1 teaspoon almond extract
¾ cup sliced almonds

Combine frosting ingredients and beat until smooth. Add milk as needed for spreading consistency. While warm, frost pastry so each portion is partially covered. Frosting will not totally cover pastry. Sprinkle with almonds.

COLD-OVEN POPOVERS
"Impressive but easy!"

YIELD: 12

3 eggs
1 cup milk

1 cup flour
½ teaspoon salt

Generously grease muffin tins with margarine. Place in coldest part of refrigerator while preparing batter.

Combine all ingredients. Mix with wire whisk, disregarding lumps. Fill muffin tins three-fourths full. Place in a cold oven. Turn temperature to 450.° Bake for 20 minutes; do not peek. Turn oven to 400° and bake for 10 minutes. Serve immediately.

FANTASTIC FRENCH TOAST
SERVES: 4

6 eggs
⅔ cup fresh orange juice
2 Tablespoons Grand Marnier
⅔ cup milk
3 Tablespoons sugar
¼ teaspoon vanilla
¼ teaspoon salt

grated peel of 1 orange
8 slices French bread,
　¾ inch thick
¼ cup butter
powdered sugar
fresh orange slices
warm maple syrup

In a large bowl, beat eggs. Add orange juice, Grand Marnier, milk, sugar, vanilla, salt and orange peel. Mix thoroughly.

Dip bread slices into egg mixture, turning to coat. Transfer to shallow dish. Pour remaining egg mixture over bread slices. Cover and refrigerate overnight.

In a large skillet, melt half the butter. Saute bread slices in batches, turning to brown about 8 minutes on each side. To serve, cut bread slices diagonally; sprinkle with powdered sugar. Garnish with orange slices and pass syrup.

BREAKFAST CREPES
YIELD: 16

1½ cups flour
1 Tablespoon sugar
¼ teaspoon salt
2 eggs

1½ cups milk
melted butter for cooking
powdered sugar
fresh lemon juice

Mix flour, sugar and salt. Whisk in eggs and milk to make a smooth, thin batter. If necessary, add additional milk.

Heat an 8-inch skillet over medium heat. Lightly coat inside of pan with buttered pastry brush. Place enough batter in skillet to cover bottom by quickly rotating pan. Return to heat; cook until slightly brown on both sides. Do not over cook.

Remove from pan. Sprinkle 1 heaping teaspoon powdered sugar over crepe. Sprinkle with fresh lemon juice; roll into cylinder. Sprinkle top lightly with powdered sugar.

BUTTERHORNS
YIELD: 3 dozen

"Marvelous with morning coffee!"

Pastry

2 cups sifted flour
1 cup butter, softened
1 egg yolk
¾ cup sour cream

¾ cup sugar
1 teaspoon cinnamon
½ cup chopped nuts

Powdered Sugar Glaze

1 cup powdered sugar
2 Tablespoons butter, softened
¼ cup half-and-half

Cream flour with butter. Mix in egg yolk and sour cream. Divide dough into thirds and wrap each third in plastic wrap. Refrigerate overnight.

Combine sugar, cinnamon and nuts.

Roll each portion of dough into an 8-inch circle. Sprinkle with one-third of the topping. Cut into 12 wedges. Roll up each wedge, starting at the wide end. Place point-side down on a greased baking sheet. Bake at 350° for 20-25 minutes. Cool. Combine glaze ingredients. Drizzle on Butterhorns.

LEMON HERB LOAF
YIELD: 1 loaf

"A delicious aroma!"

1 loaf Italian or French bread
1 cup butter, softened
2 Tablespoons minced
   green onions
½ teaspoon Italian seasoning

½ teaspoon garlic powder
¼ teaspoon marjoram
1 teaspoon grated fresh
   lemon peel
1 teaspoon fresh lemon juice

Slice bread vertically ¾ inch thick. Combine remaining ingredients. Spread butter mixture on one side of each slice. Wrap in aluminum foil. Bake at 350° for 20 minutes.

HERB BREAD
YIELD: 1 loaf

½ cup butter, softened
2 teaspoons garlic powder
½ teaspoon summer savory
1 teaspoon celery salt
½ teaspoon rosemary
½ teaspoon thyme
½ teaspoon chervil

½ teaspoon sweet basil
1 teaspoon sage
1 Tablespoon chopped
   fresh parsley
½ teaspoon oregano
1 loaf French bread, split
   in half horizontally

Combine all ingredients except bread. Spread herb butter on cut surfaces of bread. Wrap each piece in foil. Bake at 350° for 30 minutes.

FRY BREAD

YIELD: 1 dozen

"Yummy!"

vegetable oil for frying
2 cups white or whole
   wheat flour
2 teaspoons baking powder

1 teaspoon salt
⅔ cup warm water
honey

In a large skillet or deep fryer, heat oil to 400°

Combine flour, baking powder and salt. Mix in ½ cup warm water. Continue adding water to form a soft dough.

Divide dough into 12 equal portions. Roll out each portion on a floured surface until ¼ inch thick. Deep fry in hot oil until golden brown. Drain on paper towel. Serve with honey.

NOTE: Fry bread may become a Navajo Taco by layering it with cooked pinto beans, cooked ground beef, chopped onion, chopped tomato, shredded lettuce, grated Colby Longhorn cheese and taco sauce.

JOHNNY CAKE

YIELD: 9 squares

"A sweet cornbread!"

2 Tablespoons butter, softened
½ cup sugar
1 egg
1 cup buttermilk
¾ cup corn meal

1¼ cups flour
½ teaspoon baking soda
1 teaspoon baking powder
1 teaspoon salt

Cream butter and sugar. Add egg, buttermilk and corn meal, beating well.

Combine flour, soda, baking powder and salt. Add to batter; mix well. Pour into greased and floured 8-inch square pan. Bake at 400° for 25 minutes.

Before scalding milk, rinse the saucepan to be used in cold water to make cleanup easier.

ENTRÉES

WINFIELD SCOTT STRATTON discovered gold in the
Cripple Creek Independence mine. Immediately thereafter,
he gave up his modest life as a carpenter to assume a more
intriguing one as a philanthropist, eccentric and recluse.
Over the years, Stratton gave the city of Colorado Springs
a trolley line (the most advanced in the country at the time),
a public park and a fleet of bicycles for city laundresses.
He also funded emergency aid for the city of Cripple
Creek after a disastrous fire devastated the boom town
in 1896. When he died at age 54, Stratton left most of
his remaining millions for the building and maintenance
of a home for needy children and old people. Named for
his father, the Myron Stratton Home still serves today as
a haven for the needy and as a memorial to the enigmatic
gold king who endowed it.

ENTREES

*Found elsewhere in the book.

DI ENTRE

ENGLISH BEEF STEW
SERVES: 6

"Fabulous!"

1/4 cup flour
1 teaspoon salt
1/8 teaspoon pepper
1/2 teaspoon ginger
2 pounds beef chuck, cut into
   1-inch cubes
1/4 cup vegetable oil
1 Tablespoon chili sauce
1 16-ounce can stewed tomatoes

1 1/4 cups sliced fresh
   mushrooms
1 Tablespoon Worcestershire
   sauce
2 Tablespoons brown sugar
2 Tablespoons red wine vinegar
2 cloves garlic, minced
1 bay leaf
1 green or red pepper, chopped

Combine flour, salt, pepper and ginger; coat beef cubes. In a Dutch oven, heat oil. Brown beef on all sides.

Combine remaining ingredients and pour over beef. Cover tightly. Bake at 300° for 3 hours or until beef is tender.

NOTE: Serve in Yorkshire Pudding (see page 117).

STEAK AU POIVRE
SERVES: 4

"For special company!"

Brown Sauce
1 clove garlic, cut
2 14 1/2-ounce cans beef broth
1/2 cup chopped fresh mushrooms

2 sprigs fresh parsley
2 Tablespoons arrowroot
1/4 cup cold water

Rub a heavy saucepan with the garlic; discard garlic. Add broth, mushrooms and parsley; bring to a boil. Reduce heat and simmer for 15 minutes. Combine arrowroot and water, stirring until dissolved. Whisk into broth mixture. Cook, stirring constantly, until thickened. Strain before using.

Steak
1 1/2 Tablespoons cracked
   black pepper
4 4-ounce beef filets
1/4 cup butter

2 Tablespoons vegetable oil
3 Tablespoons Cognac
1 cup brown sauce

Press pepper into filets; season lightly with salt.

In a large skillet, melt 2 tablespoons butter with the oil. Cook filets until done as desired. Remove to a warm oven. Deglaze skillet with Cognac. Add brown sauce, whisking to combine with pan juices. Whisk in 2 tablespoons butter. Serve steaks with sauce.

WIENER SCHNITZEL

SERVES: 4

"A simple entree!"

1 pound veal, thinly sliced
2 lemons
⅓ cup flour
2 eggs, beaten with 2
   Tablespoons milk

1½ cups dry bread crumbs
2 Tablespoons butter
1 Tablespoon olive oil
4 iceberg lettuce leaves

Sprinkle cutlets with the juice of half a lemon. Allow to marinate for 10 minutes. Season to taste.

Dip cutlets into flour; shake off excess. Dip into egg-milk mixture, then dip into crumbs. Allow to dry on waxed paper for 5 minutes.

In a heavy skillet, heat butter and oil. Brown cutlets for 2 minutes on each side. If needed, add more butter and oil. Serve cutlets arranged on a crisp lettuce leaf garnished with lemon wedges.

CUTLETS WITH MORNAY SAUCE

SERVES: 6

Mornay Sauce

5 Tablespoons butter
3 Tablespoons flour
1¼ cups half-and-half

½ cup grated Parmesan cheese
1 Tablespoon sherry
dash freshly grated nutmeg

In a saucepan, melt 3 tablespoons butter. Stir in flour and cook for 2 minutes. Whisk in half-and-half, cheese, sherry and nutmeg. Stir until thickened; keep warm.

Cutlets

6 veal, pork or chicken
   cutlets, flattened
garlic salt
2 eggs beaten with 2
   Tablespoons water

2 cups fresh bread crumbs
2 Tablespoons vegetable oil
1 tomato cut into 6 thin slices
1 avocado, peeled and cut
   into 6 thin slices

Season cutlets with garlic salt. Bread cutlets by dipping into egg mixture, then into crumbs. Saute over medium heat in oil and 2 tablespoons butter until tender and golden. Place on a warm platter and top each cutlet with a slice of tomato and avocado. Spoon Mornay Sauce over each cutlet; brown under broiler.

TORTILLA ROJA
"Serve with San Luis Frijoles!"

SERVES: 6-8

1 pound ground beef
2 cloves garlic, minced
1 medium onion, chopped
6 Tablespoons butter
6 Tablespoons flour
3 cups chicken stock or broth
1 Tablespoon chili powder
½ teaspoon oregano
½ teaspoon sage
½ teaspoon cumin

12 flour tortillas
3 cups grated Colby
   Longhorn cheese
2 large tomatoes, peeled
   and chopped
½ head iceberg lettuce,
   finely sliced
1 8-ounce carton sour cream
1 11-ounce jar salsa roja

In a skillet, brown beef, garlic and onion; drain well. Season to taste.

In a saucepan, melt butter. Add flour and cook for 2 minutes. Whisk in chicken stock, chili powder, oregano, sage and cumin. Cook and stir until sauce thickens. Season to taste. Pour two-thirds of sauce into skillet with ground beef; mix well.

Divide meat mixture evenly between tortillas. Top each tortilla with ¼ cup cheese and a spoonful of chopped tomato. Roll tortilla and place seam-side down in a lightly greased 9 x 13-inch pan.

Spoon remaining sauce over tortillas. Bake covered at 350° for 20 minutes. Serve with a generous sprinkling of lettuce and a dollop of sour cream. Pass salsa roja.

GRILLED CHUCK ROAST

SERVES: 6

3 pounds beef chuck roast,
   cut 2 inches thick
2 Tablespoons vegetable oil
1 Tablespoon Worcestershire
   sauce
1 teaspoon salt

¼ teaspoon pepper
¼ teaspoon garlic powder
⅓ cup red wine vinegar
¼ cup catsup
2 Tablespoons soy sauce
1 teaspoon prepared mustard

Place roast in a shallow baking dish. Thoroughly combine remaining ingredients and pour over roast. Refrigerate for 5-6 hours, turning occasionally. Grill until done as desired, basting with the marinade.

71

PINEAPPLE BURGERS   SERVES: 4

½ cup brown sugar
½ cup catsup
2 Tablespoons prepared
    mustard

1 pound lean ground beef
1 8-ounce can pineapple
    rings, drained

In a saucepan, combine sugar, catsup and mustard. Simmer for 3 minutes; set aside.

Divide meat into 8 thin patties. Place a pineapple ring between 2 patties, sealing edges. Broil or grill hamburgers until done as desired. Serve with sauce.

CHINESE BEEF WITH PEPPERS   SERVES: 6
"Serve with steamed rice!"

1½ pounds beef sirloin steak,
    partially frozen
2 green peppers
1 bunch green onions
1 clove garlic
peeled fresh
    ginger root

2 teaspoons cornstarch
3 Tablespoons cold water
3 Tablespoons peanut oil
2 Tablespoons dry sherry
2 Tablespoons soy sauce
steamed rice

Assemble all ingredients close by the stove, ready to be stir-fried. Prepare as follows:

    Slice beef into pieces ¼ inch thick and 2 inches long
    Cut green peppers in half horizontally and slice into ¼-inch strips
    Slice onions into 1½-inch long pieces
    Mince garlic
    Slice 5 pieces ginger root ⅛ inch thick
    Combine cornstarch and water

In a wok or large skillet, heat 1 tablespoon oil. Add green pepper and stir-fry for 1 minute. Place in a large bowl in a warm oven.

Heat 1 tablespoon of oil in wok; add green onions and stir-fry for 1 minute. Add to the bowl in the oven.

Heat remaining tablespoon of oil in wok; stir-fry garlic and ginger root until light brown. Add meat in small batches and stir-fry quickly. Add to the bowl in oven. Continue until all the meat is cooked. Lower heat and return stir-fried ingredients to wok. Add sherry, soy sauce and cornstarch mixture. Stir until mixture thickens.

SESAME BEEF
SERVES: 6

2 pounds beef sirloin
¼ cup sugar
2 Tablespoons vegetable oil
½ cup soy sauce
dash pepper
3 green onions, sliced
1 clove garlic, minced

¼ cup sesame seeds
1 Tablespoon flour
1 8-ounce can mushroom
  pieces, drained
steamed rice
snow peas

Thinly slice beef into 2-inch strips; remove any fat. Place in
9 x 13-inch pan.

Combine remaining ingredients; mix lightly. Pour over meat and
refrigerate overnight.

In a large, hot skillet, cook meat in the marinade until done, approximately
10 minutes. Serve with steamed rice and fresh snow peas.

WRANGLERS' BRISKET
SERVES: 8-10
"Adapts to a large gathering!"

Brisket
4 pounds beef brisket
liquid smoke
Worcestershire sauce

celery salt
garlic salt
onion salt

In a Dutch oven, sprinkle beef lightly with liquid smoke, Worcestershire and
the three flavored salts. Cover and refrigerate overnight.

Bake brisket covered at 275° for 5-6 hours. Cool for 1 hour in the
refrigerator; slice thin.

Sauce
½ cup water
¼ cup cider vinegar
2 Tablespoons sugar
1 Tablespoon prepared mustard
½ teaspoon pepper
1½ teaspoons salt
¼ teaspoon cayenne pepper

2 Tablespoons fresh lemon juice
1 small onion, chopped
¼ cup butter
½ cup catsup
2 Tablespoons Worcestershire
  sauce
1 teaspoon liquid smoke

In a saucepan, combine sauce ingredients; simmer for 30 minutes. Pour
sauce over meat and heat thoroughly.

BEEF STROGANOFF

SERVES: 4-6

"A subtle blend of flavors!"

1½ pounds beef tenderloin, cut
   into bite-size pieces
½ cup butter
¼ cup brandy
4 ounces fresh mushrooms,
   thinly sliced

2 cloves garlic, minced
3 Tablespoons flour
1¼ cups beef stock or broth
1 Tablespoon tomato paste
1 teaspoon salt
1 cup sour cream

In a skillet, saute beef in ¼ cup butter. Remove meat to platter.

Add ¼ cup butter, brandy, mushrooms and garlic to the skillet; cook for
3 minutes. Shake in the flour; cook and stir for 2 minutes. Add beef stock,
tomato paste and salt; stir until well combined and sauce has thickened.
Mix in sour cream and meat. Cook over low heat for several minutes to
blend flavors.

BEARNAISE BURGERS

SERVES: 4

"Gourmet flair!"

1½ pounds lean ground beef
¼ cup red wine
1 Tablespoon finely chopped
   chives
¾ teaspoon salt

2 English muffins, split
   and toasted
watercress
cherry tomatoes

Combine beef, wine, chives, salt and pepper to taste. Shape into 4
patties. Grill until done as desired. While burgers grill, prepare Bearnaise
Sauce (see page 117). Place each burger on half of an English muffin and
spoon sauce over meat. Garnish with watercress and cherry tomatoes.

BEEF MARINADE

YIELD: 1 cup

"Try this on flank steak!"

½ cup vegetable oil
¼ cup soy sauce
2 Tablespoons cider vinegar

3 Tablespoons honey
1½ teaspoons ginger
1½ teaspoons garlic salt

In a blender or food processor, combine all ingredients thoroughly.

NOTE: The longer you marinate, the more tender and flavorful the meat
will be.

BURGUNDY-GLAZED HAMBURGERS

SERVES: 4

2 English muffins, split
5 Tablespoons butter, softened
1 pound lean ground beef
1 teaspoon vegetable oil

2 Tablespoons sliced
  green onion
1 clove garlic, minced
½ teaspoon Dijon mustard
¾ cup Burgundy wine

Toast muffins; spread with 2 tablespoons butter and keep warm.

Shape meat into 4 patties. Brown in oil until done as desired. Transfer to toasted muffins and keep warm.

Add green onions and garlic to pan, stirring for 2 minutes. Stir in mustard and wine. Boil until reduced to half of the original quantity. Whisk in 3 tablespoons butter. Spoon sauce over hamburgers.

STEAK DIANE

SERVES: 4

"For a gala occasion!"

4 6-ounce beef tenderloin filets
1½ Tablespoons green
   peppercorns
soy sauce
olive oil
1 cup beef stock or broth
1 Tablespoon cornstarch
1 Tablespoon Dijon mustard

¼ cup butter
¼ cup minced shallots
1 Tablespoon minced
  fresh parsley
dash Worcestershire sauce
dash Cognac
3 Tablespoons heavy cream

Crush peppercorns and spread one-fourth on one side of each steak along with a few drops of soy sauce and olive oil. Refrigerate until ready to cook.

Combine stock, cornstarch and mustard; set aside.

In a heavy skillet, heat 1 tablespoon olive oil and 2 tablespoons butter. When hot, saute steaks until done as desired. Remove steaks to a warm oven. Add remaining 2 tablespoons of butter to skillet and gently saute shallots and parsley for 2 minutes. Stir in stock mixture, Worcestershire and Cognac, cooking until thickened. Stir in cream. Season to taste. Serve sauce with steaks.

ITALIAN RED SAUCE

YIELD: 1½ quarts

4 cloves garlic, finely minced
2 Tablespoons olive oil
2 28-ounce cans Italian-style
  crushed pear tomatoes
  in puree
2 Tablespoons grated
  Parmesan cheese
2 teaspoons sugar

1 teaspoon salt
4 teaspoons oregano
1 teaspoon basil
¼ teaspoon pepper
¼ teaspoon thyme
¼ teaspoon tarragon
½ teaspoon celery salt
1 bay leaf

In a large kettle, saute garlic in oil. Add remaining ingredients; simmer over low heat for 30-45 minutes or until reduced to desired thickness.

NOTE: Best if prepared 24 hours in advance. Recipe may be doubled. Freezes well. It is good for pizza, lasagna and spaghetti. Onions may be added when used for spaghetti.

ITALIAN MEAT BALLS

SERVES: 6

"Mama Mia!"

2 thick slices French bread
¼ cup milk
1 egg
1 pound lean ground beef
4 ounces Italian sausage,
  without casing
6 Tablespoons grated
  Parmesan cheese

2 Tablespoons chopped
  fresh parsley
3 cloves garlic, finely minced
1 teaspoon grated fresh
  lemon peel
¼ teaspoon ground allspice
1 teaspoon salt
¼ teaspoon pepper
vegetable oil for frying

In a bowl, tear the bread into small pieces. Add the milk; toss and allow to soak for 5 minutes. Add all remaining ingredients, combining thoroughly. Form into meat balls and chill. Film a large skillet with oil. Cook meat balls until thoroughly done. Serve with spaghetti and Italian Red Sauce (see above).

SKIER STEW
SERVES: 8

"Great one-dish meal!"

2 pounds beef stew meat, cut
  into 1-inch cubes
5 carrots, peeled and sliced
  ¼ inch thick
4 celery stalks, sliced
  ¼ inch thick

7 small stewing onions, peeled
1 29-ounce can tomato sauce
2 cups water
3 Tablespoons tapioca
2½ teaspoons salt
1 Tablespoon sugar

In a heavy casserole, mix all ingredients. Cover and bake at 300° for 4-5 hours, stirring occasionally.

Just before serving, increase heat to 350°. Top stew with Dumplings.

Dumplings
1 cup sifted flour
2 teaspoons baking powder
¼ teaspoon salt

½ cup milk
2 Tablespoons vegetable oil

Sift dry ingredients together. Combine milk and oil; add to dry ingredients, stirring just to moisten. Drop from a large tablespoon atop bubbling stew. Cover and cook for 12-15 minutes.

ZUNI SUCCOTASH
SERVES: 4

"Serve with Squaw Bread!"

2 Tablespoons vegetable oil
1 pound beef round steak, cut
  into ¾-inch cubes
½ teaspoon salt
rounded ¼ teaspoon pepper

2 cups fresh string beans,
  cut into thirds
2 cups fresh or canned
  whole kernel corn
⅓ cup shelled sunflower seeds

In a Dutch oven, heat oil and brown beef cubes. Add salt, pepper and water to cover. Cover and bake at 250° for 3 hours or until meat is tender with 2-3 cups broth remaining.

Remove Dutch oven to stove top. Add beans, corn and sunflower seeds. Simmer until vegetables are tender-crisp. Adjust seasonings.

BEEF TENDERLOIN WITH SAUCE CLARET   SERVES: 6
"Easy company cuisine!"

2 ¼ pounds beef tenderloin
7 ½ Tablespoons butter
1 Tablespoon olive oil
8 green onions, sliced
8 ounces fresh mushroom caps,
    sliced ¼ inch thick

¼ teaspoon salt
freshly ground black pepper
1 cup claret
2 Tablespoons cornstarch
1 cup beef stock or broth

Season beef. In a roasting pan, heat 1 ½ tablespoons butter and the olive oil; brown beef. Roast at 350° for 40-50 minutes for medium rare. Allow to rest for 10 minutes before slicing.

In a saucepan, saute onions and mushrooms in 6 tablespoons butter for several minutes. Add seasonings. Add wine and boil for 3 minutes. Combine cornstarch and stock. Whisk into wine mixture, stirring until thickened. De-grease roasting pan and stir pan drippings into the sauce. Allow sauce to simmer gently to blend flavors. If necessary, whisk in additional cornstarch to thicken or add extra stock to thin. Slice meat ¼ inch thick; arrange on a platter. Add the juices from the meat to the sauce. Adjust seasonings. Serve sauce with meat.

BEEF ROLLS   YIELD: 3 rolls
"For the gourmet backpacker!"

5 pounds ground beef
1 ½ Tablespoons garlic salt
4 ½ teaspoons mustard seed

4 ½ teaspoons coarse pepper
2 teaspoons liquid smoke

In a large bowl, mix all ingredients. Place in a heavy plastic bag. Refrigerate for 3 days, kneading meat each day. On the fourth day, divide meat into thirds and make rolls. Place on a rack over a baking pan and bake at 150° for 8 hours. Chill before slicing.

NOTE: Freezes well.

To make edible shells, heat 4 inches of oil to 375°. Lay an egg roll wrapper or small flour tortilla on the surface of the oil. Press in center with a ladle until it is completely submerged. Without removing ladle, fry 1-2 minutes until golden brown. Remove from oil and drain on paper towels.

FILET TONINI

SERVES: 4

¼ teaspoon garlic powder
½ teaspoon salt
1½ teaspoons crushed black
 peppercorns
4 6-ounce beef tenderloin filets
3 Tablespoons vegetable oil
1 small onion, minced
1 large green pepper,
 thinly sliced

2 large red peppers,
 thinly sliced
1 clove garlic, minced
2 teaspoons curry powder
½ teaspoon paprika
1 beef bouillon cube dissolved
 in ¼ cup hot water
1½ cups heavy cream
2 Tablespoons brandy

Mix garlic powder, salt and 1 teaspoon crushed black peppercorns.
Press seasonings into steaks.

In a large skillet, heat oil. Brown steaks quickly until done as desired and
remove to a platter. Place in a warm oven.

Over low heat, add onion, pepper strips and garlic. Saute lightly. Stir in
curry, paprika, ½ teaspoon crushed black peppercorns, bouillon cube
mixture and cream. Allow sauce to reduce to desired thickness. Return
steaks to sauce. Heat brandy; pour over steaks and ignite. Spoon sauce
over meat until flames die.

CHIMICHANGAS

SERVES: 6

"A real meal!"

1 pound ground beef
1 medium onion, chopped
1 clove garlic, minced
1 8-ounce can stewed tomatoes
½ teaspoon salt
¼ teaspoon pepper
1 teaspoon oregano
1 4-ounce can diced green chilies

12 large flour tortillas
vegetable oil for frying
condiment choices:
 salsa
 sour cream
 chopped lettuce
 grated Colby Longhorn cheese
 chopped tomato
 guacamole (see page 11)

In a skillet, brown beef, onion and garlic. Drain liquid. Add tomatoes, salt,
pepper, oregano and chilies. Simmer for 20 minutes or until most of the
liquid evaporates.

Place 3 tablespoons of meat mixture on each tortilla. Fold in sides of the
tortilla; roll to make a cylinder. Secure with a wooden pick.

Deep fry chimichangas in 375° fat until golden brown. Drain on paper
towels. Keep warm in 350° oven. Serve with condiments.

ITALIAN MEAT LOAF WHIRL
"Rave reviews!"

SERVES: 8

2 pounds lean ground beef
2 eggs
1 cup fresh bread crumbs
2 Tablespoons finely
  minced onion
1 teaspoon oregano

⅛ teaspoon cayenne pepper
1 teaspoon garlic salt
1 8-ounce can tomato sauce
3 ounces Italian dry salami,
  thinly sliced
8 ounces mozzarella cheese,
  grated

Combine beef, eggs, bread crumbs, onion, oregano, cayenne, garlic salt and half of the tomato sauce. On a sheet of waxed paper, pat meat into a 10 x 16-inch rectangle. Leaving a 1-inch margin on all sides, arrange salami slices in 5 rows; sprinkle on the cheese. Beginning with the short side, roll up the meat jellyroll fashion, lifting the roll with the paper. Seal ends and edges, pressing meat together. Place seam-side down in a 9-inch loaf pan. Bake at 350° for 1 hour.

Remove from oven; drain liquid. Top with remaining tomato sauce; bake for 15 minutes. Drain liquid and allow to sit for 15 minutes before removing and slicing.

NOTE: Use leftovers to make Italian sandwiches!

TEXAS CASSEROLE

SERVES: 12

2 pounds ground beef
3 cloves garlic, minced
1 16-ounce can tomato sauce
1 teaspoon sugar
1 teaspoon salt
1 8-ounce package cream
  cheese, softened

5 green onions, sliced
1 8-ounce carton sour cream
1 12-ounce package medium
  noodles
6 ounces fresh mushrooms,
  sliced
⅔ cup grated mild Cheddar
  cheese

In a large skillet, saute beef and garlic. Add tomato sauce, sugar, salt and pepper to taste; set aside.

Combine cream cheese, onions and sour cream; set aside.

Cook noodles and drain.

Grease a 9 x 13-inch casserole. Layer it with half the noodles, half of the meat mixture, half the mushrooms and half of the cream cheese mixture. Repeat, topping with the Cheddar cheese. Bake at 350° for 30-40 minutes. Allow to stand 10 minutes before serving.

FLANK STEAK ITALIANO

SERVES: 6

"Great for bleu cheese lovers!"

2½ pounds beef flank steak
⅔ cup prepared Italian-style
   salad dressing
4 ounces bleu cheese, crumbled

3 Tablespoons butter, softened
2 green onions including tops,
   finely sliced

Trim steak and pierce both sides with a fork. Place in shallow glass pan and cover with dressing. Cover and refrigerate for 5 hours or overnight.

Combine cheese, butter and onions; set aside. Line broiler pan with foil. Place meat on foil and broil for 4-5 minutes on each side or until done as desired. Remove and spread with cheese mixture. Broil for 1 minute.

BARBECUED BEEF

SERVES: 8

"Popular with everyone!"

3 pounds beef chuck roast
1 large onion, finely chopped
½ cup red wine vinegar
2 Tablespoons sugar
1 teaspoon salt

½ cup finely sliced celery
2 teaspoons horseradish
1 14-ounce bottle catsup
½ cup water
toasted hamburger buns

Trim meat and cut into 3-inch pieces. In a casserole, combine meat with remaining ingredients except buns. Cover and bake at 300° for 4-5 hours. Mash with a potato masher to shred fine. Serve on buns.

MOUNTAINEERS' SLOPPY JOES

SERVES: 6-8

"For Saturday night supper!"

1 pound ground beef
1½ cups chopped onions
¼ cup chopped green pepper
¼ cup sliced celery
1 8-ounce can tomato sauce
¼ cup catsup

1½ teaspoons Worcestershire
   sauce
1 Tablespoon sugar
1 Tablespoon cider vinegar
½ teaspoon salt
⅛ teaspoon pepper
toasted hamburger buns

In a skillet, saute beef; drain liquid. Add remaining ingredients except buns; mix well. Cover and simmer for 30 minutes. Serve on toasted hamburger buns.

CHICKEN CURRY

SERVES: 8

"For a fun, informal dinner!"

2 frying chickens or 4 whole
   chicken breasts, split
½ cup butter
3 large onions, thinly sliced
2 teaspoons ginger
7 medium cloves garlic
2 cups water
2 teaspoons turmeric
2 teaspoons curry powder
1 Tablespoon salt
1 Tablespoon ground cumin

½ teaspoon pepper
1 teaspoon chili powder
10 cardamom seeds or
   ½ teaspoon ground cardamom
10 whole cloves
4 bay leaves
2 3-inch sticks of cinnamon
1¼ cups plain yogurt
2 apples
steamed rice
condiments (see below)

Skin chicken. If using fryers, cut into pieces.

In a large Dutch oven, melt the butter. Add half of the sliced onions and saute until limp.

In a blender, puree remaining onions, ginger, garlic and water; add to Dutch oven. Add turmeric, curry powder, salt, cumin, pepper, chili powder, cardamom, cloves, bay leaves and cinnamon. Stir in yogurt. Add chicken pieces. Cover and bake at 350° for 3 hours.

Remove from oven; allow to cool slightly. Remove chicken from bone. Cut into bite-size pieces and return to Dutch oven. Peel, core and dice apples; add to curry and heat thoroughly.

Serve with steamed rice and bowls of condiments. Suggested condiments: sliced bananas, chutney, peanuts, coconut, chopped green onions, raisins or plain yogurt.

NOTE: This is a great party dish because it may be made in advance and allows the guests to create their own entree.

ORANGE-GLAZED CORNISH HENS

SERVES: 4

4 Cornish game hens
⅓ cup brown sugar
⅓ cup sugar
1 Tablespoon cornstarch

1 Tablespoon grated fresh
   orange peel
1 cup orange juice
¼ teaspoon salt

Season hens with salt and pepper. Place breast-side up in a roasting pan. In a saucepan, combine remaining ingredients. Cook until thickened. Baste hens with glaze. Bake at 350° for 1¼-1½ hours, basting every 15 minutes. Serve with remaining glaze.

ENCHILADAS CON POLLO

SERVES: 4-6

"Chicken enchiladas!"

1 small onion, chopped
2 Tablespoons vegetable oil
1 clove garlic, minced
1 cup tomato puree
1 4-ounce can diced green chilies
2 cups cooked, cubed chicken
½ teaspoon salt
2 cups heavy cream
1 chicken bouillon cube

10-12 corn tortillas
vegetable oil for frying
4 ounces Monterey Jack cheese,
  grated
1 avocado, peeled and pitted
1 2¼-ounce can sliced
  ripe olives
salsa

Saute onion in oil until soft. Add garlic, tomato puree, chilies, chicken and salt. Simmer, stirring occasionally, for 8 minutes. Set aside.

Heat cream with the bouillon cube. Set aside.

Fry tortillas quickly in ¼ inch hot vegetable oil. Do not allow to crisp. Remove to paper towels.

Dip tortillas into cream mixture. Place 2 tablespoons of the chicken filling on each tortilla and roll up. Arrange seam-side down in a greased 9 x 13-inch baking dish. Pour remaining cream over enchiladas. Top with cheese and bake at 350° for 30 minutes. Serve garnished with avocado slices and olives. Pass salsa.

COMPANY CHICKEN

SERVES: 6

"Just terrific!"

4 whole chicken breasts; split,
  skinned and boned
½ cup chili sauce
1 teaspoon curry powder

¼ teaspoon pepper
½ teaspoon salt
1 cup heavy cream
freshly cooked linguini

Make ½-inch slashes on chicken. Place chicken pieces in a deep, buttered baking dish. Mix chili sauce, curry powder, pepper and salt; spread over chicken. Cover and refrigerate for 2 hours.

Bake uncovered at 375° for 15 minutes. Pour cream over chicken and bake for 20 minutes. Serve with freshly cooked linguini.

CHICKEN CORDON BLEU

SERVES: 8

4 whole chicken breasts; split,
  skinned and boned
8 thin slices boiled ham
8 thin slices Swiss cheese
white pepper
flour

4 eggs, beaten
4 cups seasoned croutons,
  crushed
vegetable oil for frying
fresh lemon wedges
fresh parsley sprigs

Place each chicken breast between waxed paper and pound until ¼ inch thick. Season to taste.

Place a slice of ham on each chicken breast, leaving ½ inch of chicken exposed. Place a cheese slice on top of ham, leaving ½ inch of ham exposed. Beginning at the narrow edge, tightly roll the chicken breast. Secure the end with a wooden pick, weaving it flat against the breast.

Place flour, eggs and crouton crumbs in separate shallow bowls. Dredge chicken breasts into flour, dip into egg and then into crumbs. Place on waxed paper and allow to dry for 10 minutes.

In a large skillet, cook chicken in ¼ inch hot oil until brown on all sides and done. Serve with lemon wedges and garnish with parsley.

CHICKEN WITH APPLES AND MUSHROOMS

SERVES: 4

2 whole chicken breasts, split
6 Tablespoons butter
1 Tablespoon vegetable oil
2 medium-size tart apples,
  peeled and sliced

4 ounces fresh mushroom
  caps, sliced
½ teaspoon tarragon
¼ cup apple brandy

Lightly salt, pepper and flour chicken. In a skillet, brown chicken in 3 tablespoons of the butter and the oil. Cover pan and lower heat. Cook until done, about 20 minutes. Remove chicken to a warm oven. Discard fat from skillet.

In the same skillet, melt 3 tablespoons butter; scrape up pan drippings. Add apples, mushrooms and tarragon. Cover and cook over low heat until apples are almost soft. Do not over cook. Season to taste. Return chicken to skillet. Heat apple brandy; add to chicken. Flame, spooning sauce over the chicken.

LITTLE LONDON CHICKEN PIE
SERVES: 6

"Academy cadets love it!"

Pastry
½ cup butter, softened

1½ cups flour

1 egg

2 Tablespoons ice water

Make pastry by cutting the butter into the flour. Mix in egg and enough ice water to form a ball. Wrap in plastic wrap. Chill.

Creamed Chicken
2½ quarts water

1 whole chicken

1 clove garlic, halved

4 black peppercorns

1 stalk celery

1 large onion, studded with
   4 whole cloves

1 Tablespoon salt

3 carrots, peeled and sliced
   ¼ inch thick

1 medium onion, chopped or
   6 small boiling onions

3 medium potatoes, peeled
   and diced

½ cup butter

½ cup flour

½ cup fresh or frozen peas

5 large fresh mushrooms, sliced

1 egg yolk

1 Tablespoon heavy cream

In a large pot, place water, chicken, garlic, peppercorns, celery, onion and salt. Cover and simmer for 40 minutes or until chicken is done.

Remove chicken from stock. Bone and cut into bite-size pieces. Strain and de-grease stock. Return stock to heat and add carrots, boiling onions and potatoes; cook until tender. With a slotted spoon, remove vegetables and set aside. Reserve stock.

In a large saucepan, melt butter; stir in flour and cook for 2 minutes. Whisk in 4 cups reserved stock, cooking until sauce thickens. Add chicken, reserved vegetables, peas and mushrooms. Season to taste. Pour into a greased 9 x 13-inch baking dish.

Roll out pastry to an 11 x 15-inch rectangle. Cover dish with crust. Fold crust under to make a double edge and flute edges. Cut steam vents. Combine egg yolk and cream; brush pastry with mixture. Bake at 400° for 30 minutes or until the crust is golden brown.

To reduce a sauce, cook uncovered.

CHICKEN PARMESAN
SERVES: 4
"Serve with White Spaghetti!"

Tomato Sauce
½ cup chopped onion
1 clove garlic, minced
2 Tablespoons olive oil
1 16-ounce can Italian tomatoes

3 Tablespoons tomato paste
1 teaspoon sweet basil
1 teaspoon sugar
½ teaspoon salt

In a saucepan, saute onion and garlic in olive oil. Stir in the remaining ingredients. Simmer, stirring occasionally, for 20 minutes. Puree.

Chicken
½ cup bread crumbs
⅓ cup grated Parmesan cheese
1 teaspoon oregano
¼ teaspoon salt
⅛ teaspoon pepper

2 whole chicken breasts; split, skinned and boned
2 eggs, beaten
olive oil
4 thin slices mozzarella cheese

Combine bread crumbs, Parmesan cheese, oregano, salt and pepper. Place on waxed paper. Dip chicken into beaten egg, then into crumb mixture. Let dry on waxed paper for 10 minutes.

Film a large skillet with olive oil. Saute chicken until golden brown, about 3 minutes on each side. Remove to oven-proof platter. Place 1 slice of mozzarella cheese on each piece of chicken. Spoon on sauce. Place under broiler until cheese melts.

CHICKEN IN CHAMPAGNE
SERVES: 4

1 frying chicken, quartered
¼ cup butter
2 ounces brandy
1 Tablespoon chopped fresh parsley

2 shallots, chopped
½ cup Champagne
¾ cup heavy cream

Season chicken with salt and pepper. In a skillet, brown chicken in butter until golden.

Heat brandy. Pour over chicken and ignite. Shake skillet until flames die. Add parsley, shallots and Champagne. Cover and cook over medium heat until chicken is tender, about 25 minutes.

Remove chicken to a warm oven. Whisk cream into skillet and reduce sauce until slightly thickened. Adjust seasonings. Serve sauce with chicken.

CHICKEN WITH ARTICHOKE HEARTS
SERVES: 8

4 whole chicken breasts; split,
  skinned and boned
1 14-ounce can artichoke
  hearts, halved
¼ cup butter
¼ cup flour
½ teaspoon salt
¼ teaspoon pepper

1¼ cups chicken stock or broth
1 cup half-and-half
¾ cup grated Parmesan cheese
2 Tablespoons dry sherry
¾ teaspoon rosemary
2 Tablespoons chopped
  fresh parsley

Arrange chicken in a greased 9 x 13-inch casserole. Distribute artichoke hearts over the chicken.

In a saucepan, melt butter. Stir in flour, salt and pepper and cook for 2 minutes. Whisk in stock and half-and-half; stir until mixture thickens. Add cheese, sherry and rosemary, stirring until cheese is melted. Pour sauce over chicken. Bake at 350° for 30 minutes. Garnish with parsley.

LEMON CHICKEN
SERVES: 4

⅓ cup flour
2 teaspoons paprika
2½ teaspoons salt
1 3-pound whole chicken,
  cut into pieces
⅓ cup butter

¼ cup fresh lemon juice
2 Tablespoons minced onion
1 Tablespoon vegetable oil
½ teaspoon pepper
½ teaspoon thyme
1 clove garlic, minced

In a plastic bag, combine flour, paprika and 2 teaspoons salt. Shake chicken pieces in flour mixture, coating well.

In a baking pan, melt butter. Dip chicken in butter, coating on all sides. Arrange pieces in a single layer, skin-side down. Bake at 375° for 20 minutes.

Combine remaining ingredients with ½ teaspoon salt. Turn chicken and pour the lemon mixture over pieces. Bake for 20 minutes.

SAVORY CHICKEN AND PIMIENTO ROMA   SERVES: 6
"As pretty as it is delicious!"

flour, seasoned with salt
  and pepper
1 fryer, cut up or 3 whole
  chicken breasts, split
¼ cup olive oil
1 large clove garlic, minced
½ cup minced fresh parsley
½ teaspoon poultry seasoning
½ teaspoon salt
dash Tabasco sauce
1 cup white wine

1 2½-ounce can sliced
  ripe olives
4 ounces fresh mushrooms,
  sliced
1 4-ounce jar sliced pimientos
1 8-ounce package thin
  spaghetti
½ cup butter
⅓ cup grated Parmesan cheese
chopped fresh parsley

Place the seasoned flour in a paper bag. Add chicken, a piece at a time, and shake gently to coat. Brown in hot olive oil.

Mix garlic, ½ cup minced parsley, poultry seasoning, salt, Tabasco and wine. Pour over browned chicken. Simmer for 3-5 minutes.

Transfer chicken and sauce to a baking pan and sprinkle olives, mushrooms and pimiento over chicken. Cover and bake at 350° for 35 minutes or until tender.

Cook spaghetti in salted, boiling water until al denté; drain. Toss with small pieces of butter. Garnish with Parmesan cheese and parsley. Serve as a side dish with the chicken.

SESAME FRIED CHICKEN   SERVES: 4
"Crispy!"

1 egg
¼ cup milk
¾ cup flour
¾ teaspoon baking powder
1½ teaspoons salt
1 teaspoon paprika

¼ teaspoon pepper
¼ cup sliced almonds
2 Tablespoons sesame seeds
¼ cup butter
2 Tablespoons vegetable oil
2 whole chicken breasts, split

In a shallow bowl, combine egg and milk. In another shallow bowl, mix flour, baking powder, salt, paprika, pepper, almonds and sesame seeds.

In a 9 x 13-inch baking dish, melt butter. Add oil.

Dip chicken into egg mixture and then into flour mixture, coating well. As pieces of floured chicken are placed in pan, turn once to coat with butter mixture. Bake skin-side down at 350° for 20 minutes. Turn and bake 20 minutes or until done.

CHICKEN BREASTS SUPREME
SERVES: 6

½ cup flour
2½ teaspoons salt
1 teaspoon paprika
3 whole chicken breasts; split,
  skinned and boned
3 Tablespoons butter
1 teaspoon cornstarch

¾ cup half-and-half
2 Tablespoons dry sherry
½ teaspoon grated fresh
  lemon peel
1½ teaspoons fresh lemon juice
½ cup grated Swiss cheese
parsley sprigs

In a shallow container, combine flour, salt and paprika. Dredge chicken in flour mixture, shaking off excess.

In a large skillet, cook chicken in butter, approximately 10 minutes or until done. Arrange in baking dish and place in warm oven.

Mix cornstarch with half-and-half; stir into drippings in skillet. Cook, stirring over low heat. Add sherry, lemon peel and lemon juice; stir until thickened. Pour over chicken. Sprinkle with cheese and place under broiler until cheese is melted. Garnish with parsley sprigs.

CHICKEN WITH WALNUTS AND BROCCOLI
SERVES: 6

⅓ cup dry sherry
⅓ cup soy sauce
1 Tablespoon sugar
3 Tablespoons cornstarch
⅓ cup cold water
3 whole chicken breasts; split,
  skinned and boned
½ teaspoon salt

4 fresh broccoli spears
6 Tablespoons peanut oil
1 cup walnut pieces
1 teaspoon peeled, minced
  fresh ginger root
2 cloves garlic, minced
steamed rice

In a small bowl, mix sherry, soy sauce, sugar, 2 tablespoons cornstarch and cold water. Set aside.

Cut chicken into ½-inch pieces. Sprinkle with 1 tablespoon cornstarch and salt. Set aside.

Remove broccoli flowerets and diagonally slice tender portion of stems ⅛ inch thick. Steam or simmer broccoli for 3-4 minutes. In a wok or skillet, heat 2 tablespoons oil. Quickly stir-fry broccoli in oil over high heat for 3 minutes or until tender-crisp. Remove and keep warm.

Add 2 more tablespoons oil to wok and stir-fry walnuts over moderate heat until golden. Drain on paper towels.

Add remaining 2 tablespoons oil to wok and stir-fry the ginger and garlic. Add chicken, a small amount at a time, and fry over high heat until the chicken changes color. Pour the sherry-soy sauce mixture over chicken and heat until liquid boils and thickens. Stir in walnuts and broccoli. Serve with steamed rice.

CHICKEN SCHNITZEL

SERVES: 2-3

"A family treasure!"

2 whole chicken breasts; split,
  skinned and boned
1 cup bread crumbs or saltine
  cracker crumbs
1 egg

2 Tablespoons butter
2 Tablespoons vegetable oil
1 lemon
1 clove garlic, minced (optional)

Pound chicken breasts until ¼ inch thick. Slice into ¾ inch strips.

Place crumbs in one pie plate and beat the egg in another. Dip chicken pieces first into egg and then into crumbs. Let dry for several minutes on waxed paper.

In a large skillet, heat butter and oil. Saute chicken for 2-3 minutes on each side. Remove to platter and keep warm. Serve with fresh lemon wedges or mix the juice of one lemon with an equal amount of water. Add this liquid to the skillet with garlic. Boil, scraping up drippings, and pour over chicken.

TARRAGON CHICKEN

SERVES: 6

3 whole chicken breasts; split,
  skinned and boned
⅓ cup flour
6 Tablespoons butter
4 shallots, minced

½ cup dry white wine
1½ Tablespoons tarragon
1 cup chicken stock or broth
½ cup half-and-half

Salt and pepper chicken; dredge in flour. Shake off excess and reserve remaining flour. In a large skillet, melt 4 tablespoons butter. Add chicken and brown on both sides, cooking until done. Remove to a warm oven.

Add shallots to skillet and saute lightly. Add wine and cook, stirring until liquid is almost evaporated. Whisk in reserved flour and cook for 2 minutes. Add tarragon and chicken stock, stirring constantly until well blended. Whisk in cream. Stir in 2 tablespoons butter. Pour over chicken.

To freeze casseroles, line a dish with heavy-duty aluminum foil; place the food in it, seal and freeze. When frozen, lift out the package, seal securely, label and return to freezer.

CHICKEN SPAGHETTI CASSEROLE
SERVES: 18

"Perfect for a crowd!"

3-4 pounds chicken, cooked
  and cubed
1½ pounds bulk Italian sausage,
  cooked and drained
1 medium onion, chopped
1 large green pepper, chopped
¾ cup butter
8 ounces fresh mushrooms,
  sliced
1 6-ounce can ripe olives, sliced

¾ cup flour
4 cups milk
8 ounces Old English
  cheese, grated
8 ounces American
  cheese, grated
garlic powder
1 16-ounce package spaghetti
4 ounces grated Parmesan
  cheese

Prepare meats; set aside.

In a skillet, saute onion and green pepper in ¼ cup butter. Stir in mushrooms and olives, cook for 2 minutes. Set aside.

In a saucepan, melt ½ cup butter. Stir in the flour and cook for 2 minutes. Whisk in milk and cook until thickened. Add Old English cheese and American cheese; stir until melted. Season to taste with salt, pepper and garlic powder. Combine the onion mixture with sauce.

Cook spaghetti al denté; drain. Combine with meats and sauce. Pour into a large, greased casserole; sprinkle with Parmesan cheese and bake at 350° for 40 minutes.

NOTE: This freezes very well.

WHITE PORT CHICKEN
SERVES: 6

"Serve with Creamed Leeks!"

3 whole chicken breasts; split,
  skinned and boned
3 cups sliced fresh mushrooms

1 cup white port
1 cup beef stock or broth
½ cup butter

In a large skillet, place chicken breasts, mushrooms, port and stock. Cover and simmer for 6-8 minutes. Remove breasts to platter. Using a slotted spoon, place one-sixth of the mushrooms on each breast. Cover and keep warm.

Boil remaining liquid until reduced to ½ cup. Reduce heat. Add butter 1 tablespoon at a time, stirring constantly. Adjust seasonings. Top and surround breast with sauce.

GRILLED LAMB   SERVES: 8

1 5-pound leg of lamb, boned and butterflied	½ teaspoon cracked black pepper
1 16-ounce carton sour cream	½ teaspoon oregano
2 teaspoons salt	½ teaspoon dried parsley
	½ teaspoon garlic powder

Trim lamb. Combine remaining ingredients and coat the lamb with the marinade. Cover and refrigerate for several hours or overnight. Grill over charcoal until medium rare, approximately 20 minutes on each side.

EGG ROLLS   YIELD: 16-20
"Great for hors d'oeuvres as well as for a main course!"

1 Tablespoon cornstarch	4 medium-size fresh mushrooms, chopped
2 Tablespoons chicken stock or broth	3 cups finely sliced celery
3 Tablespoons peanut oil	2 teaspoons salt
12 ounces ground pork	8 ounces fresh bean sprouts
1 Tablespoon dry sherry	16-20 egg roll wrappers
1 Tablespoon soy sauce	1 egg, beaten
½ teaspoon sugar	vegetable oil for frying
8 ounces raw shrimp, diced	

In a small bowl, mix cornstarch and chicken stock. Set aside.

In a large skillet or wok, heat 1 tablespoon oil over high heat. Add pork and stir-fry until meat loses its reddish color. Add sherry, soy sauce, sugar, shrimp and mushrooms. Stir-fry until shrimp are pink. Transfer mixture to a bowl. In the same skillet or wok, heat remaining 2 tablespoons oil. Stir-fry celery for 5 minutes. Add salt and bean sprouts. Return pork-shrimp mixture to pan, stirring until all ingredients are well combined. Add cornstarch mixture, stirring until liquid has thickened slightly. Cool mixture to room temperature.

To assemble, place approximately ¼ cup filling diagonally across the center of each egg roll wrapper. Lift lower triangular flap over the filling, tucking the point under the filling. Fold the end flaps over the filling. Brush the remaining triangular flap with beaten egg; roll and seal. Deep fry egg rolls at 375° for 5 minutes or until golden brown. Drain on paper towels. Serve with Hot Mustard Sauce (see page 106), Sweet and Sour Sauce (see page 105), or Won Ton Sauce (see page 105).

NOTE: Egg rolls may be kept warm for 1 hour in a 350° oven or reheated at 450° for 10 minutes.

ESCALLOPED BACON
"A great brunch recipe!"

YIELD: 8 slices

1 egg
2 Tablespoons milk
¼ teaspoon dry mustard
freshly ground pepper

¾ cup crushed Ritz crackers
 (about 15 crackers)
8 strips lean bacon

In a shallow bowl, beat egg; add milk and seasonings. In another shallow dish long enough to hold the bacon, place the cracker crumbs. Dip each bacon strip into egg mixture and then into crumbs, turning to coat each side.

Place bacon on a broiler pan. Bake at 300° for 10-15 minutes until lightly browned. Drain excess grease. Turn and bake 10-15 minutes. Remove from pan and drain on paper towels.

NOTE: Bacon may be prepared to cooking stage and refrigerated one day before serving.

CHINESE SESAME PORK

SERVES: 6

½ cup soy sauce
⅓ cup honey
¼ cup dry sherry
¼ teaspoon garlic powder

¼ teaspoon ginger
2 pounds pork tenderloin
2 Tablespoons dry mustard
⅓ cup sesame seeds, toasted

In a shallow dish large enough to hold the pork, blend the soy sauce, honey, sherry, garlic powder and ginger. Add pork to the marinade, turning to coat. Cover and refrigerate overnight, turning occasionally.

Remove pork, reserving marinade, and lay on a rack placed over a pan of water. Roast at 325° for 30 minutes. Turn and roast 30 minutes or until meat thermometer in thickest part of the meat reads 185°. Cool. Wrap and refrigerate for 1 hour.

Prepare dipping sauce by adding dry mustard to ½ cup of reserved marinade. Cut pork into ¼-inch slices. Serve meat at room temperature, first dipping pork into sauce and then into sesame seeds.

NOTE: Use fondue plates for a fun presentation of this entree. This may also be used as a buffet hors d'oeuvre.

PORK TOSTADA   SERVES: 10-12

1 pound dry pinto beans
3 pounds pork roast, trimmed
2 quarts water
½ cup chopped onion
2 cloves garlic, minced
1 Tablespoon salt
2 Tablespoons chili powder
1 Tablespoon cumin
1 teaspoon oregano
1 4-ounce can diced green chilies

condiments:
  chopped tomato
  chopped avocado
  chopped green onion
  thinly sliced iceberg lettuce
  grated Colby Longhorn cheese
  taco sauce
  sour cream
vegetable oil for frying
2 dozen corn tortillas

In a Dutch oven, place beans, pork roast, water, onion, garlic, seasonings and chilies. Cover and simmer for 5-6 hours. Shred roast with a fork; remove bone. If necessary, uncover and cook until most of the moisture evaporates.

Prepare desired condiments and set aside.

In a skillet, place ⅛ inch vegetable oil. Quickly fry tortillas on both sides in hot fat. Drain on paper towels. To serve, spoon pork mixture onto each tortilla and layer with desired condiments.

POSOLE   SERVES: 10

1½ pounds pork loin
2 cloves garlic, minced
2 Tablespoons vegetable oil
2 29-ounce cans hominy
1 teaspoon salt

1 teaspoon oregano
1-2 Tablespoons crumbled
  chili pequin
juice of 1 lime

In a kettle or Dutch oven, brown pork and garlic in oil. Add water to barely cover; simmer covered until pork falls off the bone. Remove bone and discard. Add remaining ingredients; simmer for 30 minutes. Adjust seasonings and de-grease Posole before serving.

NOTE: A great side dish for a Mexican meal or as a main dish accompanied by flour tortillas. Freezes well.

MOIST STUFFED PORK CHOPS

SERVES: 6

Stuffing

¼ cup margarine
1 clove garlic, minced
½ cup finely chopped onion
½ cup finely chopped celery
4 slices stale bread made
  into crumbs
2 Tablespoons chopped
  fresh parsley

½ cup chopped fresh
  mushrooms
½ cup chopped tart apple
½ cup raisins
¾ teaspoon salt
1½ teaspoon marjoram
⅛ teaspoon pepper

In a skillet, melt margarine; saute garlic, onion and celery until tender.
Stir in remaining stuffing ingredients; set aside.

Chops

6 rib pork chops, 1¼ inches
  thick
½ cup flour
½ teaspoon salt

2 Tablespoons butter
2 Tablespoons vegetable oil
1 cup apple cider or white wine

Cut a pocket in each chop, cutting from fat side almost to the bone edge.
Stuff chops with stuffing mixture and close opening with wooden picks.

Combine flour and salt; dredge chops in flour mixture. In a skillet, melt
butter with oil; brown chops on both sides. Remove chops to a baking pan.
Deglaze skillet with cider. Pour pan drippings into baking pan. Bake at
350° for 50-60 minutes. Remove chops from pan; thicken pan drippings
for gravy.

PORK TENDERLOIN A LA CRÈME

SERVES: 6

2 1-pound pork tenderloins
dry mustard
3 Tablespoons butter
¼ teaspoon rosemary

½ cup currant jelly
1 cup sour cream
1 Tablespoon flour
steamed rice

Rub the tenderloins with salt, pepper and dry mustard. In a baking pan,
brown meat in butter. Add rosemary and jelly. Cover and bake at 325° for
30-40 minutes.

Combine sour cream and flour. Whisk mixture into baking pan. Continue
baking uncovered for 15 minutes. Serve with steamed rice.

SWEET AND SOUR PORK

SERVES: 4

1 20-ounce can pineapple
   chunks
½ cup brown sugar
2 Tablespoons cornstarch
¼ cup white vinegar
2½ Tablespoons soy sauce
½ teaspoon salt

1½ pounds pork tenderloin,
   cubed
2 Tablespoons shortening
½ small onion, sliced
1 medium green pepper,
   cut into strips
steamed rice or fried rice

Drain pineapple, reserving syrup. In a saucepan, combine sugar and
cornstarch; add reserved pineapple syrup, vinegar, soy sauce and salt.
Cook and stir until thickened.

In a skillet, brown pork in shortening; cook until done. Add onion and
green pepper; cook until tender-crisp. Pour sauce over the pork mixture.
Add pineapple. Cook and stir for 1 minute. Serve with steamed rice or
Fried Rice (see page 129).

HAM 'N' SCALLOPED POTATOES

SERVES: 8-10

"Family fare!"

2 cups grated Swiss cheese
½ cup sliced green onions
1 Tablespoon dill weed
2 Tablespoons butter
2 Tablespoons flour

1 teaspoon salt
2 cups milk
7 cups cooked, peeled and
   thinly sliced potatoes
3 cups cubed ham

Toss cheese with onion and dill. Set aside.

In a saucepan, melt butter; blend in flour and salt. Cook for 2 minutes.
Whisk in milk. Bring to a boil; cook and stir for 1 minute.

In a buttered 3-quart baking dish, layer ⅓ of the potatoes, ½ of the ham,
⅓ of the cheese mixture and ½ of the sauce. Repeat, ending with the last
⅓ of the potatoes and topping with the last ⅓ of the cheese. Bake at 350°
for 30-35 minutes. Let stand for 10 minutes before serving.

HAM LOAF WITH HORSERADISH SAUCE   YIELD: 1 loaf

Ham Loaf

1 pound ham, ground
8 ounces lean pork, ground
½ cup bread crumbs
1 egg, beaten

½ cup milk
⅛ teaspoon pepper
¼ cup brown sugar
½ teaspoon dry mustard

Combine the ham, pork, bread crumbs, egg, milk and pepper. Form into a loaf and place in an 8-inch loaf pan. Mix brown sugar with mustard. Sprinkle over loaf. Bake at 350° for 1 hour. Serve with Horseradish Sauce.

Horseradish Sauce

2 Tablespoons horseradish
1 cup mayonnaise

¼ cup heavy cream

Combine sauce ingredients. Serve at room temperature with Ham Loaf.

HERBED SHRIMP   SERVES: 4-6

2 pounds medium shrimp,
  shelled and de-veined
2 teaspoons chopped
  fresh parsley
½ teaspoon tarragon
½ teaspoon ginger
1 teaspoon dry mustard
1 teaspoon seasoned salt
½ teaspoon onion salt
¼ teaspoon freshly ground
  black pepper

½ cup butter
8 ounces fresh mushrooms,
  sliced
1½ Tablespoons sliced
  green onion
1 clove garlic, minced
1 cup sliced celery
3 Tablespoons fresh lemon juice
12 cherry tomatoes
steamed rice

Prepare shrimp; set aside.

In a small bowl, combine parsley, tarragon, ginger, mustard, salts and pepper; set aside.

In a large skillet, melt butter and saute mushrooms, green onion, garlic and celery for 3 minutes. Push to the side of the skillet. Add shrimp to the skillet; sprinkle with reserved seasonings and lemon juice. Cook and stir for 2 minutes. Combine shrimp and vegetables. Cover and simmer for 3-5 minutes until shrimp are done. Do not over cook. Stir in cherry tomatoes. Serve with steamed rice.

CLAM LASAGNA

SERVES: 10

"Try it! You'll like it!"

1 10-ounce package frozen chopped spinach, thawed and squeezed dry
2 6½-ounce cans minced clams
¼ cup butter
¼ cup flour
1 8-ounce bottle clam juice
2 cloves garlic, minced
½ teaspoon sweet basil
½ teaspoon oregano
¼ cup chopped fresh parsley
3 Tablespoons fresh lemon juice
1 12-ounce package lasagna noodles
16 ounces large curd cottage cheese
8 ounces Monterey Jack cheese, thinly sliced
¼ cup grated Parmesan cheese

Prepare spinach; set aside.

Drain clams and reserve liquid. In a saucepan, melt butter. Stir in flour and cook for 2 minutes. Stir in clam juice and reserved clam liquid. Cook until thickened. Remove from heat; stir in clams, garlic, basil, oregano, parsley and lemon juice.

Cook noodles according to package directions; set aside.

Grease a 9 x 13-inch casserole and layer:
⅓ noodles
all the cottage cheese
⅓ clam sauce
⅓ noodles
all the spinach
½ Monterey Jack cheese
⅓ clam sauce
⅓ noodles
½ Monterey Jack cheese
⅓ clam sauce

Sprinkle with Parmesan cheese. Bake at 350° for 1 hour.

NOTE: May be prepared 24 hours ahead.

To make a toast box for serving a creamed dish, slice off all crusts from a loaf of unsliced bread. Slice the loaf into 3 equal cubes. Cut around inside of cube ¼ inch from the sides and no deeper than ¼ inch from the bottom. Slip knife through one side of cube ¼ inch up from bottom and cut across that one side only to release center cube of bread. Lift center cube out; discard. Completely brush box with melted butter. Place on a baking sheet. Bake at 350° for 10 minutes or until lightly toasted.

CLAM LINGUINI

SERVES: 8

¼ cup butter
½ cup olive oil
1 large onion, chopped
3 cloves garlic, minced
3 6½-ounce cans minced
  clams with juice

½ cup chopped fresh parsley
1 teaspoon oregano
¾ cup white wine
1 pound linguini
⅓ cup grated Parmesan cheese

In a saucepan, combine butter and oil; saute onion and garlic until tender. Add remaining ingredients except linguini and cheese. Simmer for 8 minutes. Season to taste.

Cook linguini in boiling salted water until al denté. Drain. Toss with the clam sauce. Serve sprinkled with Parmesan cheese.

ROCKY MOUNTAIN BAKED FISH

SERVES: 4

1 cup peeled, thinly
  sliced carrots
½ cup thinly sliced celery
¼ cup butter
2 Tablespoons flour
2 teaspoons chopped chives
½ teaspoon salt
dash cayenne pepper

1 cup milk
1 cup grated Monterey
  Jack cheese
1 pound white fish fillets
1 Tablespoon fresh lemon juice
1½ Tablespoons grated
  Parmesan cheese

In a saucepan, saute vegetables in butter for 5 minutes. Remove vegetables with slotted spoon; set aside. Blend flour and seasonings into remaining butter. Whisk in milk and cook, stirring until thickened. Add Monterey Jack cheese; stir until melted. Stir in vegetables.

Place fish in a greased baking dish. Sprinkle with lemon juice. Cover with sauce. Top with Parmesan cheese and bake at 350° for 10-15 minutes.

SCALLOPS WITH PASTA

SERVES: 6

"Worth the trouble!"

Scallop Broth

3 cups water
1 cup white vermouth
1 carrot, peeled and sliced
1 stalk celery, sliced
1 medium onion, sliced

¾ teaspoon salt
½ teaspoon thyme
white pepper
1 pound bay scallops

In a large saucepan, combine all ingredients except scallops. Bring broth to a boil; reduce to 2 cups. Add scallops and cover tightly. Remove from heat and let scallops sit for 10 minutes. Drain scallops, reserving broth. Strain broth.

Sauce

2½ Tablespoons butter
2 Tablespoons flour
2 cups scallop broth

½ cup heavy cream
⅛ teaspoon freshly
    grated nutmeg

In a saucepan, melt butter; whisk in flour. Cook for 2 minutes. Whisk in scallop broth; bring to a boil. Lower heat and simmer gently for 20 minutes. Add cream and nutmeg; season to taste. Stir in scallops and set aside.

2 cloves garlic, minced
⅓ cup minced fresh parsley
12 cherry tomatoes
½ cup butter

1 pound fettucine, cooked
    al denté
½ cup freshly grated
    Parmesan cheese

Combine garlic and parsley; set aside.

Prick each tomato with a fork to prevent bursting during cooking. In a small skillet, melt ¼ cup butter. Add tomatoes and 1 tablespoon of the parsley mixture. Cook for 1 minute; set aside.

In a pan large enough to accommodate noodles and scallops, melt remaining ¼ cup butter. Over low heat, gently stir in noodles, cheese, scallop mixture, tomatoes and remaining parsley mixture.

SAUTEED SCALLOPS

SERVES: 6

1 pound bay scallops
fresh lemon juice
white pepper
⅓ cup flour
olive oil

2 Tablespoons minced
  green onions
1 clove garlic, minced
2 Tablespoons minced
  fresh parsley
1 Tablespoon butter

Rinse scallops and dry on paper towels. Sprinkle with salt, white pepper and drops of lemon juice. Sprinkle scallops with flour and toss gently in a colander to remove any excess.

Film a large skillet with olive oil. When very hot, add scallops, tossing 4-5 minutes until lightly browned. Remove scallops. Drain oil. Saute green onion, garlic and parsley in butter for 1 minute. Return scallops to skillet and toss to coat. Serve as a first course with French bread or as a main course.

FILLET OF SOLE VERONIQUE

SERVES: 4

1½ pounds fillet of sole
1 cup milk
¼ cup butter
1 cup sliced fresh mushrooms
1 cup seedless green grapes
¼ cup flour

½ teaspoon salt
⅛ teaspoon white pepper
¼ teaspoon celery salt
¼ cup bread crumbs
2 Tablespoons grated
  Parmesan cheese

In a skillet, cover sole with milk and simmer over low heat for 5 minutes. Drain and reserve milk.

In a saucepan, melt 2 tablespoons butter; add mushrooms and cook for 3 minutes. Stir in grapes. Place mixture in a greased casserole. Place fish on top.

In the same saucepan, melt 2 tablespoons butter; blend in flour and cook for 2 minutes. Whisk in reserved milk, stirring over low heat until thickened. Add seasonings. Pour sauce over the fish and sprinkle with crumbs and cheese. Bake at 375° for 15 minutes or until hot and bubbly.

CRAB IMPERIAL
SERVES: 4
"May also be used as a fish course!"

½ cup mayonnaise
1 Tablespoon Worcestershire
  sauce
2 Tablespoons finely chopped
  green pepper
¼ cup sliced green onion tops
1 2-ounce jar chopped pimiento

½ teaspoon dry mustard
¼ teaspoon salt
1 egg
12 ounces crabmeat
⅓ cup bread crumbs
2 Tablespoons butter

In a bowl, combine mayonnaise, Worcestershire, green pepper, onion, pimiento, mustard and salt. Whisk in egg. Stir in crabmeat. Divide crab mixture among four oven-proof serving dishes. Sprinkle with crumbs and dot with butter. Bake at 350° for 20 minutes.

GOURMET OPEN-FACED SANDWICH
SERVES: any number
"A great after-the-theater supper!"

For each sandwich:
1 slice French bread
1-2 Tablespoons butter
thinly sliced dill pickle
thinly sliced tomato

thinly sliced ham
thinly sliced Swiss cheese
1 ounce dry white wine

Pan fry French bread in butter on both sides to a golden brown. Place in a baking dish. Cover bread with a thin layer of pickle, tomato, ham and cheese. Pour wine over sandwich and bake at 350° until cheese melts.

NOTE: May be prepared ahead and refrigerated. Add wine just before baking.

TUNA POCKET SANDWICHES

YIELD: 6 sandwiches

1 6½-ounce can tuna,
    drained and flaked
1 cup small curd cottage cheese
2 hard-cooked eggs, chopped
1 medium tomato, chopped
¾ cup sliced celery
2 green onions, sliced

½ cup grated mild Cheddar
    cheese
⅓ cup mayonnaise
1 teaspoon lemon pepper
¼ teaspoon salt
6 whole wheat pita breads
fresh alfalfa sprouts

In a bowl, combine all ingredients except bread and sprouts. Cut pita breads in half to form pockets. Fill each half of sandwich; top with sprouts.

THE GOLDMINER

YIELD: 2½ cups

"A sandwich with gusto!"

Thousand Island Dressing

1¼ cups mayonnaise
¼ cup chili sauce
1¼ Tablespoons minced
    green onion
1 teaspoon paprika
½ teaspoon salt

dash pepper
2 hard-cooked eggs, coarsely
    chopped
8 pimiento-stuffed green olives,
    coarsely chopped

Combine all dressing ingredients and chill.

Sandwich

pumpernickel bread
mayonnaise
thinly sliced chicken or
    turkey breast
shredded lettuce

thinly sliced tomato
thinly sliced hard-cooked eggs
thinly sliced red onion rings
crisp bacon strips

For each sandwich:
Spread a slice of pumpernickel bread with mayonnaise. Add several slices of chicken or turkey, lettuce, tomato, hard-cooked egg and onion rings. Top with strips of bacon and dressing.

CRAB AND CHEESE SANDWICH

YIELD: 6 sandwiches

3 Tablespoons butter
3 Tablespoons flour
1 teaspoon chicken bouillon
1 teaspoon dry mustard
½ teaspoon salt
1¾ cups milk

1 cup grated sharp
   Cheddar cheese
3 English muffins; split,
   toasted and buttered
12 ounces crabmeat

In a saucepan, melt butter. Blend in flour, bouillon, mustard and salt. Stir in milk. Cook, stirring constantly, for 2 minutes. Remove sauce from heat; add cheese, stirring to melt.

Arrange toasted muffin halves on oven-proof platter; top each muffin with some of the crab. Cover with cheese sauce. Broil 4-5 inches from heat until hot and bubbly but not brown.

BORDELAISE SAUCE

YIELD: 1 cup

"Serve with beef!"

2 shallots, finely chopped
2 cloves garlic, minced
2 thin slices onion
2 thin slices carrot
10 whole black peppercorns
2 whole cloves
¼ cup butter

3 Tablespoons flour
1 10½-ounce can beef broth
¾ cup Burgundy wine
½ teaspoon Bovril
2 parsley sprigs
2 bay leaves

In a saucepan, saute shallots, garlic, onion, carrot, peppercorns and cloves in butter until onion is golden. Stir in flour; cook for 2 minutes. Whisk in broth, ½ cup wine and the Bovril. Add parsley and bay leaves. Simmer for 10 minutes, stirring occasionally.

Strain sauce, discarding the vegetables and spices. Return sauce to pan. Adjust seasonings; add remaining ¼ cup wine and reheat gently. Do not boil.

When using tomatoes in a sandwich, slice from top to bottom instead of crosswise. There will be less juice to make the bread soggy.

SWEET MUSTARD SAUCE

YIELDS: 1½ cups

1 cup half-and-half
½ cup sugar
3 Tablespoons dry mustard
2 Tablespoons flour

1½ teaspoons salt
3 egg yolks
¼ cup cider vinegar

In a saucepan, combine half-and-half, sugar, mustard, flour, salt and egg yolks. Cook over medium heat, stirring frequently, until thickened. Remove from heat and stir in vinegar. Cover and refrigerate for up to 2 months. Serve with sandwiches, ham or as a dipping sauce.

SWEET AND SOUR SAUCE

YIELD: 2 cups

"Excellent for egg rolls, won tons or pork!"

1 peach, fresh or canned, minced
½ cup malt vinegar
½ cup brown sugar
1 6-ounce can unsweetened
   pineapple juice

1 Tablespoon tomato paste
juice of one orange
2 teaspoons soy sauce
2 teaspoons cornstarch

In a saucepan, combine all ingredients. Bring to a boil, stirring constantly. Reduce heat and simmer for 8 minutes. Serve at room temperature.

WON TON SAUCE

YIELD: 2½ cups

"Good for eggrolls, too!"

1 cup catsup
1 cup sugar
½ cup cider vinegar

2 Tablespoons cornstarch
   dissolved in 1 cup cold water
1 Tablespoon fresh lemon juice

Bring catsup, sugar and vinegar to a boil. Reduce heat; stir in cornstarch mixture and lemon juice. Cook until slightly thickened and clear. Serve at room temperature.

STIR-FRY GINGER SAUCE

YIELD: ¾ cup

½ cup soy sauce
¼ cup cider vinegar
1 small onion, quartered

¼-inch slice of 1-inch diameter
   fresh ginger root
1 Tablespoon cornstarch

In a blender, puree all ingredients except cornstarch. Transfer to a small saucepan and whisk in cornstarch. Simmer for 3 minutes. Serve at room temperature as a Chinese dipping sauce, or add 2-3 tablespoons of the sauce to stir-fry fresh vegetables or shrimp.

BARBECUE SAUCE

YIELD: 1¾ cups

"Spicy hot!"

¾ cup catsup
½ cup water
2 Tablespoons cider vinegar
1 Tablespoon A-1 Sauce
3 Tablespoons brown sugar

¾ teaspoon pepper
¾ teaspoon cayenne pepper
1 teaspoon chili powder
1 Tablespoon liquid smoke
½ cup finely chopped onion

In a quart jar, combine all ingredients; shake well. Prepare in advance to develop flavor. Use as a cooking sauce for pork, beef or chicken.

HOT MUSTARD SAUCE

YIELD: 1 cup

"On ham or as a Chinese dipping sauce!"

½ cup white vinegar
1 2-ounce can dry mustard

½ cup sugar
1 egg

In a small jar, combine vinegar and mustard. Cover and refrigerate overnight.

In the top of a double boiler, place mustard mixture. Add sugar and egg; mix thoroughly. Cook and stir over simmering water until thickened. Return sauce to jar; chill.

VEGETABLES

HELEN HUNT (JACKSON) discovered that the fresh dry
air and temperate climate in Colorado Springs were
beneficial to her health. She settled at the foot of Pikes
Peak to write the poems and stories for which she is famous.
Her decision to stay was made easier by her marriage to
William Sharpless Jackson. Jackson purchased a charming
cottage in Colorado Springs for his bride. It had been built
by gold king Winfield Scott Stratton when he was a carpenter.
Helen Hunt Jackson's experiences in Colorado restored
her health and revitalized her literary output. She began
laying the groundwork for the firebrand crusading she
would eventually do on behalf of the American Indian.
Ramona, the Helen Hunt Jackson novel in defense of Indian
rights, became a 19th century classic. Her writing and
campaigning for Indian causes took her away from Colorado
Springs, but she was buried in the Colorado mountains she
had always considered home.

VEGETABLES

GARDEN STUFFED TOMATOES

SERVES: 6

"Fits many menus!"

6 small tomatoes
2½ Tablespoons butter
1 medium zucchini, quartered
  and thinly sliced
4 ounces fresh mushrooms,
  sliced

3 Tablespoons chopped onion
1 clove garlic, minced
1 teaspoon salt
½ teaspoon sweet basil
2 Tablespoons grated
  Parmesan cheese

Cut a 1-inch slice from the top of each tomato; discard top. Scoop out tomato; discard core. Reserve any pulp and juice. Place tomatoes upside down on a paper towel to drain.

In a skillet, melt butter. Add tomato pulp and all remaining ingredients except cheese. Cook over high heat, stirring frequently until most of the liquid has evaporated. Spoon mixture into tomato shells. Sprinkle with cheese. Place tomatoes in a shallow baking dish. Bake at 375° for 10 minutes.

CORN FRITTERS

YIELD: 2 dozen

"These are fun!"

2 eggs, room temperature
  and separated
1 8½-ounce can cream-style
  corn

1¼ cups dry pancake mix
vegetable oil for deep frying

Beat egg yolks slightly. Stir in corn and pancake mix.

Beat egg whites until stiff; fold into corn mixture. Drop by tablespoonfuls into 375° deep fat. Cook until deep golden brown. Drain on paper towels.

STIR-FRY BROCCOLI AND CARROTS

SERVES: 6

2 Tablespoons vegetable oil
2 Tablespoons peeled, finely
   chopped ginger root
1 clove garlic, minced
1 small onion, sliced and
   separated into rings
1½ cups small
   broccoli flowerets
1 cup peeled, thinly sliced carrots

¾ cup chicken stock or broth
1 Tablespoon cornstarch
   dissolved in 1 Tablespoon
   cold water
1 8½-ounce can bamboo shoots,
   drained
1 cup sliced fresh mushrooms
2 Tablespoons oyster sauce

Have all ingredients ready by the stove. In a wok or large skillet, heat oil and stir-fry ginger root, garlic, onion, broccoli and carrots for 1 minute. Add stock, cover and cook until vegetables are tender-crisp. Add corn-starch mixture; cook and stir until thickened. Stir in bamboo shoots, mushrooms and oyster sauce. Cook and stir for 30 seconds. Season to taste.

CARROTS IN APRICOT GLAZE

SERVES: 6

"Pretty on a plate!"

1½ pounds carrots, peeled
   and sliced ¼ inch thick
1¼ cups water
1 Tablespoon sugar
¼ cup butter
¾ teaspoon salt
⅓ cup apricot preserves

¼ teaspoon freshly grated
   nutmeg
dash white pepper
grated peel of 1 small orange
fresh lemon juice
minced fresh parsley

Cook carrots in water, sugar, 1 tablespoon butter and ½ teaspoon salt until tender-crisp. Drain.

Heat and strain apricot preserves. In a skillet, melt 3 tablespoons butter. Stir in preserves, nutmeg, ¼ teaspoon salt, white pepper, orange peel and lemon juice to taste; cook until glaze consistency. Return carrots to pan and coat with glaze. Garnish with parsley.

To keep butter from burning when cooking at high heat, mix with vegetable oil in a proportion of 2 parts butter to 1 part oil.

CARROTS AND LEEKS JULIENNE
SERVES: 8

"A special dish!"

10 medium carrots, peeled
4 leeks
½ cup butter
2 Tablespoons cold water

2 teaspoons sugar
1 teaspoon salt
½ teaspoon freshly
  ground pepper

Cut carrots into julienne strips. Discard root ends and top 3 inches of leeks. Clean remaining leeks thoroughly. Cut leeks into julienne strips.

In a large skillet, place ¼ cup butter, the vegetables and remaining ingredients. Cover completely with foil, pressing it down onto the vegetables. Cook for 10-15 minutes, stirring occasionally. When vegetables are tender-crisp, add remaining butter and season to taste.

GOLD MINE CARROTS
SERVES: 8

2 pounds carrots, peeled
  and cut into julienne strips
⅓ cup brown sugar
¼ cup butter, softened

1 teaspoon salt
1 8-ounce can whole berry
  cranberry sauce

Boil or steam carrots until partially cooked; drain. In a baking dish, combine brown sugar, butter and salt. Add cranberry sauce and carrots. Bake at 350° for 15-20 minutes.

MUSHROOMS AU GRATIN
SERVES: 6

1 pound fresh mushrooms
¼ cup butter
3 Tablespoons flour
¾ cup chicken stock or broth
¼ teaspoon marjoram
1 Tablespoon chopped
  fresh parsley

¼ teaspoon salt
⅛ teaspoon pepper
½ cup heavy cream
1 Tablespoon dry vermouth
2 Tablespoons grated
  Parmesan cheese

Remove stems from mushrooms and finely chop. Slice caps.

In a skillet, melt butter; saute caps and stems. Stir in flour. Cook and stir for 2 minutes. Add stock and seasonings, stirring until thickened. Stir in cream and vermouth. Pour into buttered 1-quart casserole. Top with cheese. Bake at 350° for 15-20 minutes.

CREAMED LEEKS

SERVES: 6

"Serve with White Port Chicken!"

1½ pounds leeks   1 cup heavy cream
¼ cup butter   1 teaspoon salt

With a sharp knife, slit leeks lengthwise to within 1 inch of the root.
Under cold water, separate to thoroughly remove dirt. Discard root tip
and top 3 inches of greens. Slice remaining leeks ¼ inch thick.

In a large saucepan, melt butter. Add leeks and cook for 10 minutes,
stirring occasionally. Do not brown. Stir in cream and salt. Cook until
slightly thickened.

ONION TART

SERVES: 8

"Good even to non-onion eaters!"

¼ cup butter   1 9-inch pastry shell, baked
1½ pounds onions, thinly sliced   (see page 149)
2 eggs, beaten   4 strips bacon, cooked and
¼ cup grated Parmesan cheese   crumbled

In a skillet, melt butter and saute onions until soft. Remove skillet from
heat; mix in eggs and cheese. Pour into prepared shell and bake at 350°
for 20 minutes. Top with bacon. Serve warm or cold.

ORANGE BEETS

SERVES: 4

1 clove garlic, minced   1 medium carrot, peeled
2 Tablespoons butter   and coarsely grated
2 medium beets, peeled and   ⅔ cup orange juice
  coarsely grated

Saute garlic in butter for 2 minutes. Add remaining ingredients. Cook for
6-8 minutes, stirring occasionally. Season to taste.

SAN LUIS FRIJOLES
"Authentic!"

SERVES: A tribe

2 cups dried pinto beans
1 medium onion, diced
4 strips bacon, sliced

Sort beans, removing any that are withered or broken. Rinse remaining beans. Soak overnight in enough water to cover beans plus 2 inches.

In a kettle or crockpot, place beans, soaking water, onion and bacon. Cover and simmer gently for about 3 hours or until tender. If necessary, add more water during cooking. Season to taste.

NOTE: Quick method for soaking beans: in a large kettle, place beans in 1 quart of cold water. Cover and boil for 2 minutes. Remove from heat and let stand for 1 hour. Continue to cook as in paragraph two.

ELEGANT SPINACH

SERVES: 8

2 10-ounce packages frozen
  chopped spinach, thawed
  and squeezed dry
8 ounces fresh mushrooms
6 Tablespoons butter
1 Tablespoon flour
½ cup milk

½ teaspoon salt
⅛ teaspoon garlic powder
1 14-ounce can artichoke
  hearts, quarterd
¾ cup sour cream
¾ cup mayonnaise
3 Tablespoons fresh lemon juice

Prepare spinach; set aside.

Select several mushroom caps for garnish. Saute in 2 tablespoons butter and set aside. Slice remaining mushrooms and saute in 2 tablespoons butter. Set aside.

In a saucepan, melt 2 tablespoons butter, add flour and cook for 2 minutes. Add milk, whisking until thickened. Add salt, garlic powder, spinach and sliced mushrooms.

Arrange artichokes in the bottom of a buttered 2-quart casserole. Cover with spinach mixture. Combine sour cream, mayonnaise and lemon juice. Spread over top of spinach and arrange mushroom caps for garnish. Bake at 375° for 15-20 minutes.

111

SPINACH SAUTE

SERVES: 4

1 pound fresh spinach
2 small cloves garlic, minced
1 teaspoon peeled, minced
  fresh ginger root

2 Tablespoons vegetable oil
2 teaspoons soy sauce
¼ teaspoon salt

Wash and dry spinach. Remove stems and cut leaves into 2-inch lengths.

In a skillet or wok over moderately high heat, saute garlic and ginger root in oil for a few seconds. Add spinach, soy sauce and salt; saute for 2 minutes. Spinach should be a brilliant green. Do not over cook.

FRENCH PEAS

SERVES: 6

"Versatile dish!"

1 shallot, finely minced
¼ cup butter
2 10-ounce packages frozen
  petite peas, thawed
2 Tablespoons chopped
  fresh parsley

1 teaspoon instant
  chicken bouillon
1 teaspoon sugar
1 cup shredded iceberg lettuce

In a large skillet, saute shallot in melted butter until tender. Stir in peas, parsley, bouillon and sugar; cook for 2 minutes. Add lettuce and stir for 1 minute.

POTATOES FLORENTINE

SERVES: 8

"A contrast of colors!"

6 medium-size potatoes,
  peeled and quartered
2 teaspoons salt
¼ teaspoon white pepper
2 Tablespoons milk
1 cup sour cream
½ cup butter

2 teaspoons dried chives
¼ teaspoon dill weed
1 10-ounce package frozen
  chopped spinach, thawed
  and squeezed dry
1 cup grated mild
  Cheddar cheese

Cook, drain and mash potatoes. Add salt, pepper, milk, sour cream and butter; beat until smooth. Stir in chives, dill weed and spinach. Place in a buttered casserole. Top with cheese; bake at 400° for 30 minutes.

POTATO PANCAKES
SERVES: 6

"Tasty!"

2 ½ cups peeled, grated
  raw potatoes
¼ cup finely chopped onion
1 teaspoon salt
2 eggs, beaten
3 Tablespoons cracker crumbs
  or fine dry bread crumbs

freshly ground black pepper
butter and vegetable oil
  for frying
applesauce or sour cream

Press the excess moisture from the potatoes. Stir in onion, salt, egg
and crumbs. If the batter is too moist, add more crumbs. Add pepper
to taste.

In a large, heavy skillet, heat equal parts of butter and vegetable oil
until there is ¼ inch of fat in the skillet. Drop the pancake batter into the
hot fat by heaping spoonfuls and flatten slightly with the back of the
spoon. Fry the pancakes until crisp and brown on both sides. Drain on
paper towels and place in a warm oven until all batter is used. Serve with
applesauce or sour cream.

MACÉDOINE OF SUMMER VEGETABLES
SERVES: 6

3 Tablespoons butter
1 small onion, chopped
2 medium tomatoes, peeled
  and chopped
1 medium cucumber; peeled,
  seeded and sliced

1 medium yellow squash, sliced
1 medium green pepper, sliced
½ teaspoon cinnamon

In a large skillet, melt butter and cook onion until soft. Add remaining
vegetables and cook for 5-10 minutes. Season with cinnamon, salt
and pepper.

GOLDEN POTATO CASSEROLE
SERVES: 6

5 medium potatoes,
  peeled and cooked
½ cup chopped onion
8 ounces Velveeta cheese, cubed

½ cup mayonnaise
⅛ teaspoon pepper
6 strips bacon, cooked and
  crumbled

Slice potatoes. Mix in onion, cheese, mayonnaise and pepper; season
to taste. Place in greased casserole. Bake covered at 350° for 20 minutes.
Uncover, sprinkle with crumbled bacon and bake for 20 minutes.

SWEET POTATO BALLS
SERVES: 6

"Super accompaniment to pork!"

1 23-ounce can sweet potatoes,
  drained
¾ cup chopped dates
6 slices canned pineapple

¼ cup butter
¼ cup brown sugar
2 Tablespoons honey

Drain and mash potatoes; stir in ¼ cup dates. Shape into 6 balls.

Drain pineapple, reserving 2 tablespoons syrup. In a skillet, melt butter and stir in brown sugar, honey, reserved pineapple syrup and ½ cup dates. Heat until sugar is dissolved. Place 6 slices pineapple into glaze, and top each with a potato ball. Cover and simmer over low heat for 10-15 minutes, spooning glaze over potatoes several times during cooking.

AUTUMN BUTTERNUT SQUASH
SERVES: 8

"Delicious with ham!"

Nutty Topping
1½ cups cornflakes,
  coarsely crushed
¼ cup chopped pecans

1 Tablespoon butter, melted
¼ cup brown sugar

Gently mix all ingredients; set aside.

Squash
1 2-pound butternut squash
¼ cup butter
1½ teaspoons brown sugar
⅛ teaspoon salt

pinch white pepper
3 cups peeled and sliced
  Jonathan apples
2 Tablespoons sugar

Cut squash in half lengthwise. Scrape out seeds and membrane. Place cut-side down on foil-covered baking sheet. Bake at 350° for 45 minutes or until a knife point pierces squash easily. Scrape out pulp and beat until smooth. Season with 2 tablespoons butter, brown sugar, salt and pepper. Set aside.

In a skillet, melt 2 tablespoons butter. Add apples; sprinkle with sugar. Cover and simmer over low heat until barely tender. Spread apples in a greased 8-inch square baking dish. Spoon squash over apples. Sprinkle Nutty Topping over squash. Bake at 350° for 15 minutes or until brown.

ZUCCHINI BAKE   SERVES: 6

1 pound zucchini   5 Tablespoons butter
½ teaspoon salt   2 Tablespoons flour
1 medium onion, chopped   heavy cream
1 clove garlic, minced   ⅔ cup grated Swiss cheese

Wash zucchini and cut off ends. Place a colander in a bowl and coarsely grate zucchini into it. Toss with salt; reserve juice.

In a skillet, saute onion and garlic in 2 tablespoons butter. Stir in zucchini. Add remaining butter and stir in flour; cook for 2 minutes. Whisk in reserved juice. Cook, stirring constantly, until thickened. Add cream if needed to thin. Season to taste and stir in ⅓ cup of the cheese. Place in a buttered casserole and top with remaining cheese. Bake at 350° for 20-25 minutes.

ZUCCHINI AU GRATIN   SERVES: 4

¼ cup chopped onion   dash white pepper
1 clove garlic, minced   ¼ teaspoon dill weed
1 Tablespoon butter   8 cherry tomatoes, halved
1 pound zucchini, cubed   2 ounces mild Cheddar cheese,
¼ teaspoon salt   cut into small cubes

In a skillet, saute onion and garlic in butter. Add zucchini, salt, pepper and dill weed; cook for 5 minutes.

In a buttered 1-quart baking dish, layer half the zucchini mixture, half the tomatoes and half the cheese; repeat. Bake at 350° for 20 minutes.

SPICED SQUASH   SERVES: 6
"For Thanksgiving!"

4 medium acorn squash   salt
butter   ginger
dark brown sugar

Place whole squash on a baking sheet and bake at 350° for 45 minutes or until a knife point easily pierces squash. Cut squash in half. Remove seeds and scrape pulp from squash. Measure out pulp by cupfuls. Mash by hand or puree in food processor.

To each cup of squash puree add:
1 Tablespoon butter   ¼ teaspoon salt
1 Tablespoon dark brown sugar   ⅛ teaspoon ginger

Place squash mixture in a greased baking dish. Bake at 350° for 20-30 minutes.

INDIAN CORN PUDDING

SERVES: 8

"Instead of potatoes!"

3 eggs
1 16-ounce can cream-style
  corn
2 cups milk
½ cup yellow corn meal
1 cup grated Colby Longhorn
  cheese

½ teaspoon baking powder
2 cloves garlic, minced
1 4-ounce can diced
  green chilies
5 Tablespoons butter
1 teaspoon salt

Combine all ingredients; blend well. Pour into a greased 2-quart casserole. Place casserole in a bain marie (see page 166). Bake at 350° for 1 hour or until knife inserted in center comes out clean.

VEGETABLE MEDLEY

SERVES: 4

5 medium carrots, peeled and
  sliced
1 medium onion, sliced
3 Tablespoons butter
3 Tablespoons flour
1½ cups milk
5 ounces American cheese,
  grated

¼ teaspoon garlic powder
¼ teaspoon salt
dash pepper
1 10-ounce package frozen
  chopped spinach, thawed
  and squeezed dry

Cook carrots and onion in a small amount of salted water until tender. Drain.

In a saucepan, melt butter; add flour and cook for 2 minutes. Whisk in milk, cheese, garlic powder, salt and pepper. Cook until cheese is melted.

Place half the spinach into a greased 1-quart casserole. Add half the carrot mixture and half of the cheese sauce. Repeat layers. Bake at 350° for 20-30 minutes.

To remove cabbage leaves without tearing, immerse cabbage in warm water. The leaves will separate from the core with ease.

EGGS, PASTA AND GRAINS

SPENCER PENROSE discovered that he had a gift for making money. His investments in Cripple Creek, Utah copper processing, and various other Colorado ventures made him a very wealthy young bachelor. He maintained an interest in the flashy life until he met JULIE McMILLAN and made her his wife in 1906. Spencer and Julie brought art, music and culture to Colorado Springs. Under Spencer's direction, the Broadmoor Hotel was built and flourished. He also oversaw the construction of a road up Pikes Peak and organized the first Pikes Peak Auto Hill Climb in 1916. Other Penrose projects included the modernization of the Mt. Manitou Incline and the construction of the Will Rogers Shrine on Cheyenne Mountain. The Penroses not only donated land for the Colorado Springs Fine Arts Center, but also endowed it. Substantial endowments from the Penroses to both the community of Colorado Springs and the State of Colorado continue today through funds administered by the El Pomar Foundation.

EGGS, PASTA AND GRAINS

YORKSHIRE PUDDING

SERVES: 8

2 eggs, room temperature
1 cup milk, room temperature

1 cup sifted flour
½ teaspoon salt

Beat eggs and milk; whisk in flour and salt.

Generously grease eight 3½-inch diameter oven-proof dishes. Fill dishes half full. Place dishes on a baking sheet in a cold oven; turn temperature to 425° for 20 minutes. Turn off oven and let dishes stand in oven for 5 minutes. Serve immediately.

NOTE: For a unique presentation, fill Yorkshire Pudding with English Beef (see page 69).

HOLLANDAISE SAUCE

YIELD: 1½ cups

"The preparation makes the difference!"

4 egg yolks, room temperature
1 Tablespoon cold water
1 cup butter, room temperature

2½ teaspoons fresh lemon juice
freshly grated nutmeg
white pepper

In the top of a double boiler, beat egg yolks and water until slightly thickened.

Place double boiler top over simmering water. Add butter, 2 tablespoons at a time, beating constantly with a hand beater. Incorporate each addition well. Add lemon juice, nutmeg and white pepper to taste. This process takes 20-25 minutes. Remove from heat and beat for 1 minute.

BEARNAISE SAUCE

YIELD: 1 cup

"Serve warm or cold!"

4 egg yolks
1 Tablespoon tarragon vinegar
¼ teaspoon salt
½ cup butter, melted

1 Tablespoon chopped green
  onion or fresh chives
1 Tablespoon minced
  fresh parsley

In a blender or food processor, place egg yolks, vinegar and salt; blend well. With machine running, add butter in small amounts. Stir in remaining ingredients.

MUSHROOM OMELETTE

SERVES: 4

"For Sunday morning!"

Mushroom Sauce

3 Tablespoons butter
1 Tablespoon minced shallot
  or green onion
8 ounces fresh mushroom caps,
  sliced ⅛ inch thick

½ cup chicken or beef stock
  or broth
1½ Tablespoons flour
2 Tablespoons heavy cream
2 teaspoons chopped
  fresh parsley

In a saucepan, melt butter and cook shallots for 2 minutes. Add mushroom caps and stock. Cover and cook for 3-5 minutes. Whisk in flour and cook for 2 minutes. Stir in cream and parsley. Season to taste.

Omelette

4 eggs

2 Tablespoons butter

Prepare a 4-egg omelette by first beating eggs. In a 7-inch skillet, melt butter. When foam has subsided, add eggs. Using two forks, prong-sides down, in one hand, gently pull eggs away from sides of the pan, tilting pan so that uncooked egg moves to the outside edge. Continue in this manner until egg is cooked and bottom of omelette is lightly browned. Place three-fourths of the warm mushroom filling on half of the omelette. Fold over; remove to warm platter and surround with remaining sauce.

CHILI HUEVOS

SERVES: 6

1 7-ounce can whole green
  chilies, drained
6 ounces Colby Longhorn
  cheese, thinly sliced

6 eggs
1 Tablespoon flour

Split chilies; remove seeds and membrane. In a buttered 8-inch square pan, layer half the chilies and half the cheese; repeat.

In a bowl, whisk eggs, flour, salt and pepper to taste. Pour over chilies and cheese. Bake at 300° for 30 minutes. Turn oven off. Open oven door slightly and allow eggs to sit for 10-15 minutes.

NOTE: May be served with salsa roja and a dollop of sour cream.

CHILIES RELLENOS

SERVES: 8

"Delicioso!"

1 27-ounce can whole
   green chilies
1 pound Monterey Jack cheese,
   cut into 3 x 1 x ¼-inch strips
5 eggs
¼ cup flour
1¼ cups milk

½ teaspoon salt
⅛ teaspoon white pepper
dash Tabasco sauce
8 ounces Colby Longhorn
   cheese, grated
½ teaspoon paprika

Carefully slit one side of each chili and rinse out seeds. Lay on paper towel and pat dry. Enclose a strip of Monterey Jack cheese in each chili.

In a bowl, beat eggs; gradually add flour and beat until smooth. Whisk in milk, salt, pepper and Tabasco.

Arrange half the chilies in a greased 9 x 13-inch baking dish.

Sprinkle with half the Colby Longhorn cheese and ¼ teaspoon paprika. Repeat for second layer. Pour egg mixture over chilies. Bake at 350° for 45 minutes or until knife inserted in center comes out clean. Let stand for 15 minutes before cutting.

GREEN CHILI QUICHE

SERVES: 8

"A simple supper!"

1 9-inch pastry shell, partially
   baked (see page 149)
8 ounces spicy pork sausage
1 4-ounce can diced green
   chilies, drained
3 eggs
1 cup heavy cream

¼ teaspoon salt
¼ teaspoon pepper
1 Tablespoon finely sliced
   green onion
4 ounces Monterey Jack
   cheese, grated

Prepare pastry.

Brown sausage and drain well. Spread sausage over pastry. Spread chilies over sausage.

Beat eggs and cream. Stir in salt, pepper, onion and cheese. Pour over chilies. Bake at 375° for 30-40 minutes or until a knife inserted in the center comes out clean. Allow to stand 10 minutes before cutting.

SOUFFLÉ ROLL WITH CHICKEN-SPINACH FILLING

SERVES: 8

Soufflé Filling

3 Tablespoons butter
⅓ cup chopped onion
4 ounces fresh mushrooms,
  sliced
1 10-ounce package frozen
  chopped spinach, thawed and
  squeezed dry

1 cup cooked, diced chicken
½ cup diced ham
1 3-ounce package cream cheese
⅓ cup sour cream
1½ teaspoons Dijon mustard

In a saucepan, melt butter. Saute onion and mushrooms for 2 minutes. Stir in remaining ingredients, cooking until cheese is melted. Season to taste. Set aside.

Soufflé Roll

6 Tablespoons butter
½ cup flour
2 cups milk
½ cup grated Parmesan cheese
½ cup grated mild Cheddar
  cheese

¼ teaspoon salt
4 eggs, room temperature
  and separated
paprika

Grease a 10 x 15-inch jellyroll pan. Line bottom with waxed paper. Grease and flour paper.

In a saucepan, melt butter; stir in flour and cook for 2 minutes. Add milk, whisking constantly. Stir until mixture comes to a boil and thickens. Add cheeses and salt, cooking until cheese is melted. Remove from heat. Cool slightly. Add egg yolks, mixing well.

In a large bowl, beat egg whites until stiff but not dry. Fold a dollop of whites into soufflé base. Fold in remaining whites. Spread soufflé evenly in prepared pan. Bake at 325° for 40 minutes or until golden brown.

When soufflé is done, place another piece of greased waxed paper over soufflé and cover with a flat baking sheet; invert. Remove pan and paper immediately. Spread filling evenly over top of entire soufflé. Roll up lengthwise, using the waxed paper to support the roll. Roll onto platter seam-side down. Dust lightly with paprika.

To make a "top hat" on an unbaked soufflé, insert a knife 1½ inches from the edge of the soufflé dish, 1½ inches deep and scribe a circle.

CAMEMBERT SOUFFLÉ

SERVES: 6

"A delicate flavor!"

1 Tablespoon butter
1 Tablespoon grated Parmesan
  cheese
¼ cup diced celery
2 Tablespoons thinly sliced
  green onion
1 clove garlic, minced
3 Tablespoons butter
3 Tablespoons flour
1 teaspoon dry mustard

½ teaspoon salt
dash white pepper
1 cup milk
5 ounces Camembert cheese,
  rind removed and cheese
  coarsely diced
½ cup grated Parmesan cheese
5 egg yolks, room temperature
7 egg whites, room temperature

With 1 tablespoon butter, grease a 2-quart soufflé mold and sprinkle with 1 tablespoon Parmesan cheese to coat evenly. Shake out excess cheese.

In a saucepan, saute celery, onion and garlic in butter until tender. Stir in flour, mustard, salt and pepper. Cook for 2 minutes. Whisk in milk. Add cheeses and stir until melted. Remove from heat.

Beat egg yolks until thick. Gradually beat into cheese mixture.

In a large bowl, beat egg whites until stiff. Fold a dollop of whites into soufflé base to lighten. Fold soufflé base into whites. Turn into prepared soufflé dish (see top hat soufflé, page 120) and bake at 350° for 35-40 minutes. Serve at once.

CHEESE SPOON BREAD

SERVES: 6-8

4 cups milk
⅔ cup yellow corn meal
2 Tablespoons butter
2 cups grated mild Cheddar
  cheese

2 teaspoons salt
½ teaspoon paprika
⅛ teaspoon cayenne pepper
3 eggs, room temperature
  and separated

In a large saucepan, bring milk to a boil. Whisk in corn meal and butter, stirring constantly. Reduce heat and stir in cheese. Cook until mixture is thickened. Add salt, paprika and cayenne. Quickly whisk in egg yolks. Cook and stir for 1 minute. Allow to cool slightly.

Beat egg whites until stiff but not dry. Fold into cheese mixture. Pour into a 2-quart soufflé dish. Bake at 350° for 45-50 minutes.

MUSHROOM QUICHE

SERVES: 6

"Salad, bread and you!"

1 9-inch pastry shell, partially
   baked (see page 149)
¼ cup butter
2 Tablespoons minced shallots
12 ounces fresh mushrooms,
   sliced
1¼ teaspoons salt

⅛ teaspoon pepper
1 teaspoon fresh lemon juice
3 eggs
1 cup heavy cream
dash nutmeg
¼ cup grated Swiss cheese

Prepare pastry shell.

Melt butter and saute shallots lightly. Stir in mushrooms, salt, pepper and lemon juice. Simmer until liquid evaporates.

Beat eggs and cream with nutmeg. Stir in mushroom mixture. Pour into prepared pastry shell. Sprinkle with cheese. Bake at 375° for 30-40 minutes or until a knife inserted in the center comes out clean and top is lightly browned. Allow to stand 15 minutes before cutting.

SEAFOOD QUICHE

SERVES: 6

1 8-inch pastry shell, partially
   baked (see page 149)
2 Tablespoons minced
   green onion
3 Tablespoons butter
4 ounces cooked crab,
   shrimp or lobster

½ teaspoon salt
2 Tablespoons white vermouth
3 eggs
1 cup heavy cream
1 Tablespoon tomato paste
dash pepper
¼ cup grated Swiss cheese

Prepare pastry shell.

In a skillet, saute onion in butter for 2 minutes. Add the shellfish and ¼ teaspoon salt, stirring for 2 minutes. Add vermouth and boil until almost all the liquid evaporates. Allow to cool slightly.

In a mixing bowl, beat eggs with cream, tomato paste, ¼ teaspoon salt and pepper. Blend in the shellfish mixture; adjust seasonings. Pour into prepared shell; sprinkle with cheese. Bake at 375° for 30 to 35 minutes. Allow to stand 15 minutes before cutting.

MUSHROOM CRUST QUICHE

SERVES: 8

"A different twist!"

8 ounces fresh mushrooms,
  coarsely chopped
3 Tablespoons butter
½ cup crushed saltine crackers
½ cup sliced green onions
1 cup grated Swiss cheese
1 cup grated Monterey Jack
  cheese

1 cup small curd cottage cheese
3 eggs
¼ teaspoon salt
¼ teaspoon cayenne pepper
¼ teaspoon paprika

Saute mushrooms in 2 tablespoons butter. Stir in cracker crumbs. Turn into a 9-inch pie plate and press to form crust.

Saute onions in 1 tablespoon butter. Spread onions, Swiss cheese and Monterey Jack cheese over crust.

In a blender or food processor, combine cottage cheese, eggs, salt and cayenne until smooth. Pour over cheese. Sprinkle with paprika. Bake at 350° for 25-30 minutes. Allow to stand 10 minutes before cutting.

EGGS SUPREME

SERVES: 12

"Good potluck dish!"

¼ cup butter
¼ cup flour
1 cup sour cream
1 cup milk
¼ teaspoon thyme
¼ teaspoon marjoram
¼ teaspoon sweet basil
¼ cup chopped fresh parsley

1 pound sharp Cheddar
  cheese, grated
18 hard-cooked eggs, sliced
1 pound bacon, cooked and
  crumbled or 1 pound ham,
  cubed
1 cup seasoned stuffing mix

In a saucepan, melt butter; add flour and cook for 2 minutes. Add sour cream and milk; stir until thickened. Add herbs and cheese; cook until cheese has melted.

Arrange eggs, then bacon in a buttered 9 x 13-inch baking dish. Pour sauce over bacon and sprinkle with stuffing mix. Bake at 350° for 30 minutes.

PASTA PRIMAVERA

SERVES: 6

1 pound bulk Italian sausage
8 ounces fresh mushrooms,
   sliced
6 Tablespoons butter
3 Tablespoons olive oil
2 cloves garlic, minced
⅓ cup sliced green onions
1 medium zucchini, quartered
   and sliced
1 medium green pepper,
   coarsely chopped

1 Tablespoon chopped
   fresh parsley
½ teaspoon sweet basil
½ teaspoon oregano
12 ounces fettuccine noodles
1 cup heavy cream
⅔ cup freshly grated
   Parmesan cheese

In a skillet, cook sausage until done. Drain and set aside.

Saute mushrooms in 3 tablespoons butter; set aside. Add olive oil to skillet
and saute garlic and onions. Stir in the zucchini, green pepper, parsley,
basil and oregano. Cook until vegetables are tender-crisp. Stir in sausage
and mushrooms. Season to taste.

Cook fettuccine al denté in boiling salted water; drain.

In a large saucepan, heat 3 tablespoons butter and cream until slightly
thickened. Stir in fettuccine and cheese. Pour onto a large platter and top
with sausage mixture or thoroughly combine both mixtures before serving.

CREAMY PESTO DRESSING

YIELD: 1¾ cups

"Marvelous on freshly cooked pasta!"

1½ cups mayonnaise
1 cup lightly packed
   parsley leaves
¼ cup freshly grated
   Parmesan cheese

2 Tablespoons milk
2 Tablespoons fresh lemon juice
1 small clove garlic
1 teaspoon sweet basil

In a food processor or blender, thoroughly combine all ingredients. Cover
and refrigerate for 2 hours to blend flavors.

FETTUCCINE ALFREDO

SERVES: 4-6

"That's Italian!"

14 ounces fettuccine noodles
1 cup heavy cream
3 Tablespoons butter
⅔ cup freshly grated
   Parmesan cheese

½ teaspoon salt
freshly ground pepper
freshly grated nutmeg

Drop the fettuccine noodles into 4 quarts of boiling water that has been seasoned with 2 tablespoons of salt. Cook noodles al denté. Drain immediately.

In a kettle large enough to hold all the cooked fettuccine, simmer ⅔ cup of the cream and the butter until they have thickened slightly.

Over low heat, toss the fettuccine with the sauce. Add the remaining cream, cheese, ½ teaspoon salt, 4-6 twists of the pepper mill and 2 scrapings of nutmeg. Toss briefly until the cream has thickened and the noodles are well coated. Adjust seasonings.

WHITE SPAGHETTI

SERVES: 6-8

"Serve with Chicken Parmesan!"

3 cloves garlic, minced
½ cup butter
¼ cup olive oil
1 16-ounce package spaghetti,
   cooked al denté

3 eggs, beaten
6 ounces grated Parmesan
   cheese

In a large pot, saute garlic in butter and oil. Stir in spaghetti. Over low heat, quickly stir in the eggs and cheese.

When unable to serve cooked, drained pasta immediately, toss lightly with a small quantity of olive or vegetable oil to prevent clumping.

LASAGNA FLORENTINE

SERVES: 16

"Perfect for bring-along buffets!"

4 ounces cream cheese,
  softened
1 pound ricotta or
  cottage cheese
¼ cup sour cream
½ teaspoon oregano
1 small onion, diced
4 cloves garlic, minced
½ cup butter
6 Tablespoons flour
3 cups chicken stock or broth

12-15 lasagna noodles
2 10-ounce packages frozen
  chopped spinach, thawed and
  squeezed dry
8 ounces fresh mushrooms,
  sliced
8 ounces mozzarella cheese,
  grated
8 ounces mild Cheddar cheese,
  grated
½ cup grated Parmesan cheese

Combine the cream cheese, ricotta and sour cream. Stir in oregano, salt and pepper to taste; set aside.

In a saucepan, saute onion and garlic in butter until transparent. Add flour to make a roux and cook for 2 minutes. Whisk in stock, blending until smooth and thickened. Season to taste.

Cook noodles until al denté. Rinse in cold water and lay out individually.

Grease a 9 x 13-inch baking dish. Layer the lasagna in the following order:

1. ⅓ noodles
2. ½ cheese mixture
3. ½ spinach
4. ½ mushrooms
5. ½ Cheddar cheese
6. ½ mozzarella cheese
7. ⅓ garlic sauce
8. ⅓ noodles
9. ½ cheese mixture
10. ½ spinach
11. ½ mushrooms
12. ½ Cheddar cheese
13. ½ mozzarella cheese
14. ⅓ garlic sauce
15. ⅓ noodles
16. ⅓ garlic sauce
17. Parmesan cheese over top

Cover and bake at 325° for 1¼ hours. Remove cover and bake for 15 minutes.

MACARONI AND CHEESE
"A change from the traditional!"

SERVES: 6

3 Tablespoons butter
¼ cup minced onion
3 Tablespoons flour
2 cups milk
8 ounces mozzarella cheese,
  grated

1 2-ounce jar chopped
  pimiento
1½ cups elbow macaroni,
  cooked and drained
12 ounces bulk sausage, cooked
  and drained

In a Dutch oven, melt butter; saute onion until soft. Stir in flour and cook
for 2 minutes. Add milk; whisk until smooth. Add cheese, pimiento, salt
and pepper to taste; cook until cheese is melted. Stir in macaroni
and sausage.

POPPY SEED NOODLES

SERVES: 6

1 8-ounce package wide
  egg noodles
1 cup sour cream
1 cup small curd cottage cheese
¼ cup minced onion
1 clove garlic, minced

1 Tablespoon Worcestershire
  sauce
1 Tablespoon poppy seeds
dash Tabasco sauce
paprika

Cook noodles in boiling salted water for 5 minutes. Drain well. Fold in
remaining ingredients except paprika. Turn into a buttered baking dish;
sprinkle with paprika. Bake at 350° for 25-30 minutes.

EGG NOODLES
"Homemade is so much better!"

YIELD: 1 pound

2¾ cups flour
3 eggs

1 teaspoon salt
4-5 Tablespoons water

In the food processor bowl fitted with the steel blade, place flour, eggs, salt
and 4 tablespoons water; process for 1 minute. If necessary, add more water
so that dough forms a ball. The dough may appear to be made up of granular
particles; however, as long as it can be squeezed into a coherent mass, it
is fine. Turn dough onto work surface and knead to blend. Dough should
be firm. Divide and wrap portions in plastic wrap. Roll and cut as desired.
Cook noodles in a large quantity of boiling, salted water until al denté,
approximately 3-5 minutes.

BARLEY-MUSHROOM CASSEROLE

SERVES: 6

½ cup chopped onion
3 Tablespoons butter
1 cup pearl barley
3 cups chicken stock or broth

4 ounces fresh mushrooms,
  sliced
½ teaspoon salt
¼ teaspoon pepper

In a large saucepan, saute onion in butter until soft. Stir in barley. Cook over medium heat until the barley browns lightly.

Bring stock to a boil; add to barley. Stir in mushrooms, salt and pepper. Simmer covered over low heat until barley has absorbed all the liquid and is tender, about 50 minutes.

NOTE: For a variation, add either ⅓ cup sliced celery or ⅓ cup slivered almonds to the last 5 minutes of cooking.

SPANISH RICE

SERVES: 6

½ cup chopped onion
2 Tablespoons butter
2 cups cooked rice
1 cup sour cream
½ cup cottage cheese
1 bay leaf, crumbled

¼ teaspoon salt
dash of pepper
1 4-ounce can diced
  green chilies
1 cup grated mild
  Cheddar cheese

In a skillet, saute onion in butter. Combine with remaining ingredients except Cheddar cheese.

In a greased casserole, layer half the rice mixture and top with ½ cup Cheddar cheese; repeat. Bake at 350° for 25 minutes.

STIR-FRY RICE

SERVES: 4

"More than just rice!"

3 green onions, sliced
2 Tablespoons butter
4 cups cooked rice
1 6-ounce can shrimp
  or crabmeat

1 cup cooked, cubed ham
  or pork
3 Tablespoons soy sauce
2 eggs, slightly beaten

In a wok or skillet, stir-fry onion in butter until tender. Stir in rice, seafood meat and soy sauce. Add eggs. Cook and stir until eggs are set.

SHERRIED WILD RICE

SERVES: 8

"Something special!"

1 cup wild rice
½ cup butter
½ cup slivered almonds
2 Tablespoons finely
  chopped onion

8 ounces fresh mushrooms,
  sliced
1 teaspoon salt
2 Tablespoons sherry
3 cups chicken stock or broth

Pour 1½ quarts boiling water over the rice and let stand for 30 minutes. Drain. Pour another 1½ quarts boiling water over the rice. Allow rice to cool completely in water; drain well.

In a skillet, melt butter and stir in rice, almonds, onion, mushrooms and salt. Saute over medium heat for 5 minutes, being careful not to let almonds or onion brown. Stir in sherry.

Turn into a 2½-quart casserole. Pour chicken stock over rice. Bake covered at 325° for 1 hour and 15 minutes. Uncover and bake for 35-45 minutes or until rice is tender and liquid is absorbed.

FRIED RICE

SERVES: 6

"Serve with Chinese food!"

3 strips bacon, sliced
2 Tablespoons sliced
  green onion
2 Tablespoons chopped
  green pepper

3 cups cooked rice
2 eggs, beaten
1 Tablespoon soy sauce
¼ teaspoon salt
¼ teaspoon pepper

In a skillet, fry bacon until crisp. Add onion and green pepper, cooking for 3 minutes. Stir in remaining ingredients; cook until eggs are set.

RICE AND VERMICELLI

SERVES: 8-10

"Wonderful texture!"

4 ounces vermicelli, broken
  into small pieces
½ cup butter
3 cups rice

4 cups chicken or beef stock
  or broth
1 teaspoon salt

In a large saucepan, brown vermicelli in butter. Stir in rice and cook for 2 minutes. Add stock and salt; bring to a boil. Cover and reduce heat. Cook for 30 minutes or until rice is tender and liquid has been absorbed.

BACK COUNTRY GRANOLA BARS

YIELD: 16 bars

"An energy snack!"

½ cup butter, softened
¾ cup brown sugar
½ cup quick-cooking oats
½ cup whole wheat flour
½ cup flour
¼ cup wheat germ
1 teaspoon grated fresh
  orange peel

2 eggs
1 cup whole blanched almonds
¼ cup raisins
¼ cup flaked coconut
½ cup semi-sweet
  chocolate chips

Cream butter with ½ cup brown sugar; beat in oats, flours, wheat germ and orange peel. Pat into lightly greased 8-inch square pan.

Combine eggs, ¼ cup brown sugar, almonds, raisins, coconut and chocolate chips. Pour over crust, spreading evenly. Bake at 350° for 25-30 minutes. Cool before cutting. Wrap individually in foil for lunches or hiking.

GRANOLA

YIELD: 12 cups

"Good for you!"

2 teaspoons vanilla
⅔ cup light corn syrup
¼ cup water
⅔ cup vegetable oil
6 cups old-fashioned oats
⅔ cup shelled sunflower seeds
⅔ cup sesame seeds

⅔ cup shredded coconut
⅔ cup wheat germ
⅔ cup slivered almonds
2 teaspoons salt
⅔ cup nonfat dry milk
1½ cups raisins

In a small bowl, combine vanilla, corn syrup, water and oil.

In a large baking pan, combine all remaining ingredients except raisins. Pour corn syrup mixture over granola and toss well. Bake at 275° for 30 minutes. Turn and separate granola with a spatula; bake for 10 minutes or until golden. Cool and stir in raisins.

DESSERTS

CHARLES LEAMING TUTT, SR. came to Colorado in 1884 from Philadelphia longing to be a cowboy. After three freezing winters in the Black Forest, he moved to town to sell real estate and insurance. At this point in time, he greeted Spencer Penrose, his old friend. They cooked up many a deal together. The Cripple Creek real estate firm of Tutt and Penrose dabbled in everything. Soon the two discovered they had control over most of the Cripple Creek gold milling. Tutt also became involved in a new copper refining method in Utah. Yachting, trap and skeet shooting were among his favorite pastimes. After selling his copper milling shares to Penrose, he retired at the ripe old age of 41 with the wealth to enjoy his favorite diversions.

DESSERTS

These recipes have been tested at 6,000 feet; most of them will not be adversely affected by altitude. If you desire to make altitude adjustments, consult your state university home economics extension office.

STRIKE-IT-RICH BARS

YIELD: 4 dozen

Layer I

½ cup butter
½ cup sugar
⅓ cup cocoa
1 teaspoon vanilla
1 egg

2 cups graham cracker crumbs
1 cup flaked coconut
½ cup chopped pecans
 or walnuts

In a saucepan, combine butter, sugar, cocoa and vanilla over low heat. Add egg and cook for 5 minutes, stirring constantly. Mix in crumbs, coconut and nuts. Press into 9 x 13-inch pan. Chill for 15 minutes.

Layer II

½ cup butter, softened
2 cups powdered sugar

2 Tablespoons instant
 vanilla pudding
3 Tablespoons milk

Cream butter and sugar. Add pudding and milk. Beat until smooth. Spread over first layer. Chill for 15 minutes.

Layer III

6 ounces semi-sweet
 chocolate chips

2 Tablespoons butter
milk

Melt chocolate chips with butter. Add milk until thin enough to spread. Frost bars. Chill.

DUTCH BUTTERCAKE

YIELD: 3 dozen

"A super shortbread!"

2 cups flour
1 cup sugar
½ cup margarine
½ cup butter

2 teaspoons almond extract
1 egg
sugar for garnish

Mix flour and 1 cup sugar. Cut in margarine and butter until fine crumbs.

Mix almond extract and egg. Add to dry ingredients to make a firm dough. Press dough into greased 9 x 13-inch baking pan. Bake at 400° for 20-25 minutes. Do not over cook. Remove from oven and sprinkle with sugar. When completely cool, cut into diamond shapes.

APRICOT BARS

Apricot Bar
1 6-ounce package dried
  apricots
½ cup butter, softened
2 cups brown sugar
2 eggs
2 Tablespoons Grand Marnier

1 teaspoon grated fresh orange
  peel
1½ cups flour
1 teaspoon baking powder
¼ teaspoon salt

In a bowl, place apricots. Cover with boiling water; let stand for 15 minutes. Drain apricots well; cut into bite-size pieces. Set aside.

Cream butter with brown sugar; add eggs, Grand Marnier and orange peel. Mix thoroughly. Blend in flour, baking powder and salt; fold in apricots. Turn mixture into greased 10 x 15 x 1-inch pan. Bake at 350° for 20-25 minutes. Cool before frosting.

Orange Butter Cream Frosting
2 cups powdered sugar
4 teaspoons fresh orange juice
4 teaspoons fresh lemon juice
4 teaspoons butter, softened

1½ teaspoons grated fresh
  orange peel
½ cup finely chopped walnuts

In a mixing bowl, beat frosting ingredients except walnuts until smooth. Frost bars and sprinkle with nuts.

MUD PIE BARS

Pecan Coconut Brownie
1 cup margarine
2 cups sugar
4 eggs
2 Tablespoons cocoa
1½ cups flour

1 Tablespoon vanilla
1 cup chopped pecans
1 cup flaked coconut
1 7-ounce jar marshmallow
  cream

Cream margarine and sugar. Add eggs; beat smooth. Mix in cocoa, flour and vanilla. Fold in pecans and coconut. Pour into a greased 9 x 13-inch pan. Bake at 350° for 30-40 minutes. Cool slightly.

Spread marshmallow cream atop brownie. Place in freezer for 30 minutes. Prepare frosting.

Chocolate Frosting
½ cup margarine
¼ cup cocoa
5 Tablespoons milk

1 Tablespoon vanilla
1 pound powdered sugar

In a saucepan, combine margarine, cocoa and milk over low heat until margarine is melted. Off the heat, beat in vanilla and powdered sugar. Frosting will set up as it cools. Frost bars. Keep refrigerated.

CARAMEL BARS
"Will become a repeated recipe!"

YIELD: 2½ dozen

1 14-ounce package caramels
⅓ cup milk
1 cup flour
1 cup old-fashioned oats
½ teaspoon baking soda
¾ cup brown sugar

¼ teaspoon salt
¾ cup margarine, softened
1¼ cups semi-sweet chocolate
 chips
¾ cup cocktail peanuts

In a saucepan, melt caramels with milk.

Combine flour, oats, soda, sugar and salt. Cut in margarine until pea sized. Spread three-fourths of the oat mixture in a greased 9 x 13-inch pan. Bake at 350° for 10 minutes. Remove from oven.

Sprinkle chocolate chips and peanuts on top of crust. Drizzle caramel mixture atop. Sprinkle remaining oat mixture over all. Bake for 12 minutes. Cool completely before cutting.

CARAMEL BROWNIES
"Easy recipe for a sweet treat!"

YIELD: 2½ dozen

1 14-ounce package caramels
⅔ cup evaporated milk
1 18½-ounce package German
 chocolate cake mix
¾ cup butter, melted

1 cup chopped pecans
 or walnuts
1 cup semi-sweet
 chocolate chips

In a saucepan, melt caramels with ⅓ cup evaporated milk over low heat.

In a mixing bowl, combine cake mix, butter, ⅓ cup evaporated milk and nuts; mix well. Spread half the dough into a greased 9 x 13-inch pan. Bake at 350° for 10 minutes.

Remove from oven; sprinkle chocolate chips over baked crust. Drizzle caramel mixture atop. With hands, form remaining dough into small pancakes and place over caramel mixture. Will not cover completely. Bake for 20 minutes. Cool slightly before cutting.

For delicately browned cookies, choose shiny baking sheets. Dark surfaces absorb heat more quickly, and cookies tend to over brown on the bottom.

THREE-LAYER BROWNIES
YIELD: 1 dozen

"Everyone's favorite!"

Brownie

2 ounces unsweetened chocolate
½ cup margarine
2 eggs
1 cup sugar

½ cup flour
1 teaspoon vanilla
½ cup chopped walnuts
  (optional)

Melt chocolate with margarine; stir in remaining ingredients. Pour into a greased 8-inch square baking pan. Bake at 350° for 25-30 minutes. Cool completely.

Filling

2 Tablespoons butter, melted
1 cup powdered sugar

1½ Tablespoons half-and-half
1 teaspoon vanilla

Combine filling ingredients; spread over brownie. Chill for 10 minutes.

Glaze

½ ounce unsweetened chocolate

1 Tablespoon butter

Melt chocolate with butter. Drizzle over filling; chill.

NOTE: The brownies are fantastic by themselves! For Chocolate Chip Brownies, stir in 6 ounces semi-sweet chocolate chips before baking; omit filling and glaze.

ALMOND BROWN SUGAR BARS
YIELD: 3 dozen

7 Tablespoons butter
½ cup powdered sugar
1 cup flour
½ cup brown sugar

1 Tablespoon water
¾ teaspoon fresh lemon juice
¾ cup sliced almonds
¾ teaspoon vanilla

Cream 4 tablespoons butter and powdered sugar. Add flour and mix well. Spread into a 9-inch square pan. Bake at 350° for 12 minutes.

In a small saucepan, melt 3 tablespoons butter. Add brown sugar, water and lemon juice. Bring to a boil, stirring constantly. Remove from heat. Stir in almonds and vanilla. Remove pan from oven; spread topping over crust. Bake at 350° for 15 minutes. Cut when cool.

24 KARAT COOKIES
YIELD: 3½ dozen

1 cup shortening
¾ cup sugar
1 cup cooked, mashed carrots
1 egg
1 teaspoon vanilla
2 cups flour
2 teaspoons baking powder

½ teaspoon salt
¾ cup flaked coconut
2 cups powdered sugar
1 Tablespoon butter, softened
finely grated peel of 1 orange
fresh orange juice

In a mixing bowl, cream shortening and sugar. Beat in carrots, egg and vanilla. Stir in flour, baking powder, salt and coconut; mix well. Drop by teaspoonfuls onto a greased baking sheet. Bake at 375° for 12-15 minutes. Frost when cool.

Orange Butter Cream Frosting
To prepare frosting, combine powdered sugar, butter and orange peel. Add enough orange juice to make frosting a spreading consistency.

FROSTED CHOCOLATE DROP COOKIES
YIELD: 3½ dozen

Cookies
1¾ cups flour
½ teaspoon baking soda
½ teaspoon salt
¾ cup sugar
½ cup margarine
1 egg

2 ounces unsweetened
   chocolate, melted
½ cup buttermilk
1 teaspoon vanilla
½ cup chopped pecans

Measure flour, soda and salt. Mix well; set aside.

In a mixing bowl, cream sugar and margarine. Add egg; mix well. Stir in chocolate. Add buttermilk to chocolate mixture alternating with dry ingredients. Stir in vanilla and nuts. Drop batter by teaspoonfuls onto baking sheet. Bake at 375° for 8-10 minutes. Frost when cool.

Vanilla Butter Cream Frosting
2 cups powdered sugar
¼ cup butter, softened

½ teaspoon vanilla
2 Tablespoons heavy cream

Combine sugar, butter, vanilla and 1 tablespoon cream. Beat well. Add additional cream as needed to reach a spreading consistency.

CHOCOLATE KISS PEANUT BUTTER COOKIES

YIELD: 5 dozen

"Try the cookie without the kiss!"

1 cup margarine, softened
1 cup sugar
1 cup brown sugar
2 eggs
1½ teaspoons vanilla
1 cup peanut butter

2½ cups flour
2 teaspoons baking soda
1 teaspoon baking powder
½ teaspoon salt
5 dozen chocolate kiss candies, unwrapped

Cream margarine, sugars, eggs and vanilla. Stir in peanut butter. Combine dry ingredients; stir into creamed mixture.

Shape dough into 1-inch balls; roll in sugar. Place on baking sheet. Bake at 350° for 8-10 minutes. Remove from oven; press a chocolate kiss on top of each cookie. Bake for 2 minutes. Remove from oven; cool completely before storing.

WHOOPIE PIES

YIELD: 4 dozen

"Children love them!"

1 cup shortening
1 cup sugar
2 eggs
2 cups flour
⅔ cup cocoa
¼ teaspoon salt

1 teaspoon baking soda
⅔ cup buttermilk
½ cup water
¼ cup butter, softened
1 teaspoon vanilla
2 cups sifted powdered sugar

In a mixing bowl, beat ½ cup shortening and sugar. Add 1 egg and 1 egg yolk, reserving white.

Combine flour, cocoa, salt and soda; add alternately to sugar mixture with buttermilk and water. Drop batter by small teaspoonfuls onto baking sheet. Bake at 350° for 8-10 minutes; cool.

To prepare filling, combine butter, ½ cup shortening, reserved egg white and vanilla; gradually add powdered sugar. Beat until light. To assemble cookies, spread filling on the bottom side of one cookie and top with a second cookie. Store in refrigerator.

GINGERSNAPS
YIELD: 4 dozen
"Soft and chewy!"

¾ cup margarine, softened
1 cup brown sugar
¼ cup light molasses
1 egg
2¼ cups sifted flour

½ teaspoon ground cloves
1 teaspoon ginger
1 teaspoon cinnamon
2 teaspoons baking soda
½ teaspoon salt

In a mixing bowl, beat margarine, brown sugar, molasses and egg. Add remaining ingredients; beat well. Refrigerate for 30 minutes. Form into 1-inch balls. Roll in sugar. Place on baking sheets. Bake at 375° for 8-10 minutes. Do not over cook.

COWBOY COOKIES
YIELD: 4 dozen
"The best little chocolate chip cookie in Colorado!"

½ cup margarine
½ cup brown sugar
½ cup sugar
½ cup vegetable oil
1 egg
1 teaspoon vanilla
1¾ cups flour
½ teaspoon salt

½ teaspoon baking soda
½ teaspoon cream of tartar
½ cup chopped pecans
½ cup flaked coconut
½ cup old-fashioned oats
½ cup Rice Krispies
6 ounces semi-sweet chocolate
   chips

Cream margarine with sugars and oil. Beat in egg and vanilla. Add remaining ingredients; mix well. Drop by teaspoonfuls onto baking sheet. Bake at 350° for 8-10 minutes.

ROLLED SUGAR COOKIES
YIELD: 5 dozen
"These will become a favorite!"

1 cup butter, softened
1¼ cups sugar
1½ teaspoons vanilla
2 eggs

1 Tablespoon milk
2½ cups flour
2 teaspoons baking powder

Cream butter, sugar and vanilla. Beat in eggs and milk. Add flour and baking powder; mix well. Divide dough in half; wrap in plastic wrap and refrigerate for several hours or overnight.

Working with half the dough at a time, roll out on lightly floured surface ¼ inch thick; cut into desired shapes. If not frosting, sprinkle with sugar. Bake at 350° for 8-10 minutes. Do not brown.

NOTE: If desired, frost with Vanilla Butter Cream Frosting (see page 135).

MERINGUE KISSES
YIELD: 6 dozen

"Great for a cookie exchange!"

4 egg whites, room temperature
¼ teaspoon salt
¼ teaspoon cream of tartar
1 teaspoon vanilla

1½ cups sugar
6 ounces semi-sweet
   chocolate chips
1 cup chopped walnuts

Beat egg whites until foamy. Add salt, cream of tartar and vanilla. Continue beating until soft peaks are formed. Add sugar a little at a time, beating until stiff peaks are formed. Fold in chocolate chips and nuts.

Drop by small teaspoonfuls onto a baking sheet lined with heavy paper. Bake at 300° for 35 minutes.

NOTE: For a variation, substitute 6 ounces butterscotch chips and 1 cup chopped blanched almonds for chocolate chips and walnuts.

MELTAWAY COOKIES
YIELD: 4 dozen

"Perfect for teatime!"

1 cup butter, softened
¾ cup cornstarch
2 cups powdered sugar
1 cup flour

finely grated peel of 1 lemon
1 3-ounce package cream
   cheese, softened
few drops yellow food coloring

Cream butter with cornstarch and ½ cup powdered sugar. Blend in flour and half of the lemon peel. Chill.

Form dough into balls the size of a walnut. Bake at 350° for 10-12 minutes Do not brown. Cool on baking sheet before removing to frost.

To make frosting, thoroughly combine cream cheese with 1½ cups powdered sugar, remaining half of the lemon peel and a few drops of yellow food coloring. Frost cookies when cool.

NOTE: As a variation, add 1½ teaspoons vanilla to the cookie and 1 teaspoon vanilla to the frosting in place of the lemon peel.

GREAT GORPY COOKIES

YIELD: 4 dozen

1 cup butter, softened
1 cup brown sugar
2 teaspoons milk
1 teaspoon baking soda
2 cups flour

1 cup raisins
1 cup cocktail peanuts
¾ cup semi-sweet
   chocolate chips

In a mixing bowl, cream butter with sugar. Beat in milk and soda. Mix in flour. Stir in raisins, peanuts and chocolate chips.

Drop by teaspoonfuls onto greased baking sheets. Cookies may be placed fairly close together as they do not spread. Bake at 350° for 8-10 minutes. Cool on baking sheets for several minutes before removing from pan.

RASPBERRY DIAMOND COOKIES

YIELD: 2 dozen

"These melt in your mouth!"

1 cup butter, softened
3 Tablespoons sugar
2 cups flour

1 12-ounce jar raspberry
   preserves
1 recipe Vanilla Butter Cream
   Frosting (see page 135)

Cream butter and sugar. Add flour. Pat dough into 10 x 15 x 1-inch baking sheet. Bake at 375° for 15 minutes. Do not brown.

When cool, slice into diamond shapes by making diagonal cuts on cookie 1½ inches apart. Decorate each cookie with a strip of raspberry preserves and a strip of Vanilla Butter Cream Frosting on either side of the preserves.

MACE CAKE

SERVES: 12

"Unusual flavor!"

1 cup butter, softened
3 cups sugar
1½ teaspoons vanilla
5 eggs
3 cups sifted flour

½ teaspoon baking soda
1½ teaspoons mace
1 cup buttermilk
fresh fruit

In a mixing bowl, cream butter, sugar and vanilla. Beat in eggs, one at a time. Combine flour, soda and mace. Add to egg mixture alternately with buttermilk, beating well. Pour batter into a greased and floured 12-cup Bundt pan. Bake at 350° for 50-60 minutes. Cool for 15 minutes; turn out of pan. Serve with a combination of fresh fruits.

CAKES

OATMEAL CAKE
SERVES: 16

"Best when made ahead!"

Cake
1½ cups boiling water
1 cup quick-cooking oats
½ cup margarine
1 cup brown sugar
1 cup sugar
2 eggs

1½ cups flour
1 teaspoon baking soda
1 teaspoon cinnamon
1 teaspoon nutmeg
½ teaspoon salt

Pour boiling water over oats; set aside to soak.

In a mixing bowl, cream margarine and sugars. Beat in remaining ingredients. Pour into greased and floured 9 x 13-inch pan. Bake at 350° for 35-45 minutes. Frost cake while warm.

Broiled Frosting
¼ cup brown sugar
½ cup sugar
1 cup flaked coconut
1 cup chopped walnuts

6 Tablespoons butter
¼ cup half-and-half
¼ teaspoon vanilla

In a saucepan, combine all frosting ingredients except vanilla. Heat until bubbly and sugars are dissolved. Remove from heat; stir in vanilla. Pour over warm cake and broil until topping is nicely browned; watch carefully.

MOLASSES CAKE
SERVES: 20

"Old-fashioned!"

1½ cups butter
1½ cups dark brown sugar
4 eggs
4½ cups flour
1½ teaspoons cinnamon
1½ teaspoons ginger

½ teaspoon mace
½ teaspoon ground cloves
1½ teaspoons baking soda
1½ cups light molasses
1½ cups milk
2 cups heavy cream, whipped

Cream butter with sugar. Beat in eggs one at a time. Add molasses to butter mixture.

In another bowl, sift flour with cinnamon, ginger, mace, cloves and soda.

Add dry ingredients to butter-sugar mixture alternately with milk. Pour into a greased and floured 9 x 13-inch pan. Bake at 350° for 45-55 minutes. Cool. Serve with sweetened whipped cream.

DELUXE CHOCOLATE CAKE

SERVES: 12

"For a birthday party!"

Cake

2 ounces unsweetened chocolate
¾ cup butter
1½ cups sugar
2 teaspoons vanilla
3 eggs, room temperature
   and separated

1 teaspoon baking soda
½ teaspoon salt
2 cups sifted cake flour
1¼ cups buttermilk

Melt chocolate with butter. Beat in ¾ cup sugar, vanilla, egg yolks, soda and salt. Add flour alternately with buttermilk.

Beat egg whites until soft peaks are formed. Slowly add ¾ cup sugar; beat until stiff peaks are formed. Fold into chocolate mixture. Pour into two greased and floured 9-inch round cake pans. Bake at 350° for 25-30 minutes. Cool for 10 minutes; remove from pan. Frost cake when cool.

Chocolate Mocha Frosting

½ cup butter, softened
2 squares bitter chocolate,
   melted

1 teaspoon vanilla
3 cups powdered sugar
Hot coffee

In a mixing bowl, cream butter; add powdered sugar, one cup at a time. Add melted chocolate and vanilla. Add hot coffee to spreading consistency.

Caramel Butter Frosting

½ cup butter
1 cup brown sugar

¼ cup milk
3½ cups sifted powdered sugar

In a saucepan, melt butter; add brown sugar. Bring to a boil; stir for 1 minute or until thickened. Cool slightly. Add milk; beat smooth. Beat in enough powdered sugar to make a spreading consistency.

When preparing a chocolate cake, grease the pans, then dust with cocoa instead of flour.

CAKES

BANANA CAKE   SERVES: 12
"For a trip to the mountains!"

Cake

½ cup butter, softened
1½ cups sugar
2 eggs
1¼ cups mashed ripe bananas
2 cups flour
1 teaspoon baking powder

1 teaspoon baking soda
½ teaspoon salt
1 cup buttermilk
1 teaspoon vanilla
1 cup chopped walnuts

In a mixing bowl, cream butter and sugar. Add eggs; beat until fluffy. Beat in bananas.

Combine flour, baking powder, soda and salt. Add the flour mixture alternately with the buttermilk to the banana mixture. Fold in vanilla and nuts. Pour into a greased 9 x 13-inch pan or two 8-inch round cake pans. Bake at 375° for 30-40 minutes. Cool for 10 minutes; remove from pan. Frost cake when cool.

Banana Frosting

¼ cup butter, softened
2 cups powdered sugar

3 Tablespoons mashed ripe
  banana
1 Tablespoon fresh lemon juice

Thoroughly cream butter and sugar. Stir in banana and lemon juice.

GERMAN CHOCOLATE ROLL   SERVES: 8
"Easy! Easy!"

¼ cup butter
1⅓ cups flaked coconut
1 cup chopped pecans
1 14-ounce can sweetened
  condensed milk
3 eggs
1 cup sugar

⅓ cup cocoa
⅔ cup flour
¼ teaspoon salt
¼ teaspoon baking powder
⅓ cup water
1 teaspoon vanilla
powdered sugar

Line a 10 x 15-inch jellyroll pan with foil. Melt butter in pan; sprinkle coconut and nuts evenly. Drizzle with condensed milk.

In a mixing bowl, beat eggs for 2 minutes. Gradually add sugar, beating for 2 minutes. Add remaining ingredients except powdered sugar; blend for 1 minute. Pour batter evenly into prepared pan. Bake at 375° for 15 minutes or until cake springs back when touched in center.

Remove from oven. Sift powdered sugar over cake; cover with towel. Invert; remove pan and foil. Starting with 10-inch side, roll cake up jellyroll fashion using the towel to aid. Leave towel over roll while cooling.

MOULE AU CHOCOLATE

SERVES: 12

"A molded chocolate cake!"

3 ounces unsweetened chocolate
6 Tablespoons butter
¼ cup water
3 eggs, room temperature
   and separated

1 teaspoon vanilla
¾ cup sugar
¼ cup flour

Generously butter a 4-cup savarin or ring mold. Melt chocolate with butter and water over lowest heat. Transfer to a large bowl. Beat in egg yolks one at a time, beating well after each addition. Add vanilla, sugar and flour. Beat for 3 minutes.

Beat egg whites until stiff but not dry. Fold into chocolate mixture. Pour into mold. Place in a bain marie (see page 166). Bake at 375° for 40 minutes. Remove mold from water bath; cool in pan for 5 minutes. Cake will fall. Unmold by running a sharp-edged knife around edges. Invert onto serving plate; remove mold. Cool completely.

Garnish

1 cup heavy cream
¼ cup powdered sugar

½ teaspoon vanilla
semi-sweet chocolate shavings

Whip cream until stiff; fold in sugar and vanilla. Spoon into center of mold. Sprinkle cream with chocolate shavings. To serve, cut into thin slices and serve with a portion of cream.

COCONUT POUND CAKE

SERVES: 16

"Oh, yum!"

1 cup butter, softened
½ cup shortening
3 cups sugar
6 eggs
½ teaspoon almond extract

1 teaspoon coconut flavoring
3 cups flour
1 cup milk
1 cup flaked coconut

In a mixing bowl, cream butter, shortening and sugar. Add eggs, one at a time; beat well after each addition. Add flavorings. Add flour and milk alternately; beat well. Stir in coconut. Spoon batter into a greased and floured 12-cup Bundt or tube pan. Bake at 350° for 50-60 minutes. Allow to stand for 10 minutes before removing from pan.

NOTE: For a variation, add 1 teaspoon vanilla, 1 teaspoon lemon extract and 1 teaspoon salt in place of the almond and coconut flavorings and coconut.

COINTREAU POUND CAKE

SERVES: 12

Cake

1 cup butter, softened
2 cups sugar
6 eggs
2 cups flour

¼ cup fresh orange juice
1 teaspoon almond extract
1 teaspoon lemon extract
⅓ cup Cointreau

Cream butter and sugar. Add eggs, one at a time; mix well after each addition. Gradually add flour; beat for 5 minutes. Add orange juice and extracts.

Pour into greased and floured 12-cup Bundt pan. Bake at 350° for 50-60 minutes. Allow to stand for 10 minutes. Remove from pan; pierce top with wooden pick. Spoon Cointreau over top of cake, allowing it to be absorbed. When cool, drizzle cake with Orange Glaze or sprinkle with powdered sugar.

Orange Glaze

2 Tablespoons fresh orange
   juice, warmed
1 cup sifted powdered sugar

1 teaspoon grated fresh orange
   peel

Combine all ingredients. If necessary, thin with additional orange juice.

PUMPKIN JELLYROLL

SERVES: 10

3 eggs
1 cup sugar
⅔ cup canned pumpkin
1 teaspoon fresh lemon juice
¾ cup flour
1 teaspoon baking powder
2 teaspoons cinnamon
½ teaspoon nutmeg

½ teaspoon salt
1 cup chopped pecans
1½ cups powdered sugar
2 3-ounce packages cream
   cheese, softened
2 Tablespoons butter, softened
½ teaspoon vanilla

In a mixing bowl, beat eggs on high speed for 3 minutes; gradually add sugar. Stir in pumpkin and lemon juice.

Combine flour, baking powder, cinnamon, nutmeg and salt; fold into pumpkin mixture. Pour into greased and floured 10 x 15 x 1-inch pan. Sprinkle with nuts. Bake at 375° for 15-18 minutes.

Turn out onto a tea towel that has been sprinkled with ½ cup powdered sugar. Begin with narrow side and roll up towel and cake together. Cool for 15-20 minutes.

Prepare filling by thoroughly combining 1 cup powdered sugar, cream cheese, butter and vanilla. Gently unroll cake and spread with filling; reroll cake. Chill.

BLACK FOREST CAKE
SERVES: 16

"A European favorite!"

Cake

2 ¼ cups flour
1 ⅔ cups sugar
⅔ cup cocoa
1 ¼ teaspoons baking soda
1 teaspoon salt

¼ teaspoon baking powder
1 ¼ cups water
¾ cup shortening
2 eggs
1 teaspoon vanilla

Grease and flour two 9-inch round cake pans.

In a large mixing bowl, combine all cake ingredients. Beat on high speed for 3 minutes. Pour into prepared pans and bake at 350° for 30-35 minutes.

Cherry Filling

1 16-ounce can pitted red
  tart cherries
½ cup sugar

3 Tablespoons cornstarch
¼ cup Kirsch

Drain cherries; reserve liquid.

In a saucepan, combine sugar, cornstarch and enough water added to cherry liquid to measure ¾ cup. Cook, stirring constantly, until mixture thickens and boils for 2 minutes. Stir in Kirsch and cherries. Chill.

Icing

3 cups heavy cream
⅔ cup powdered sugar
chocolate curls

Beat cream until stiff. Fold in sugar. To assemble cake, spread bottom layer of cake with half of the cherry filling and 2 cups of whipped cream. Place second layer on top; spread remaining cherry filling. Ice top and sides of cake with remaining whipped cream. Decorate with chocolate curls. Chill.

To make chocolate curls, draw a potato peeler across a bar of chocolate. Best results occur when chocolate is slightly warm.

BROWNIE CAKE

YIELD: 4 dozen

'For chocolate lovers!"

1 cup butter
2½ cups sugar
4 eggs
2 teaspoons vanilla
1 cup plus 2 Tablespoons flour

1 16-ounce can chocolate syrup
⅓ cup milk
1 6-ounce package semi-sweet
   chocolate chips

In a mixing bowl, beat ½ cup butter, 1 cup sugar, eggs and 1 teaspoon vanilla. Add flour and syrup, mixing well. Pour into a greased 11 x 17 x ¾-inch baking sheet. Bake at 350° for 15-20 minutes.

In a saucepan, heat ½ cup butter, 1½ cups sugar and milk. Boil for 1 minute without stirring. Remove from heat; stir in chocolate chips. With a mixer, beat 3-5 minutes or until frosting is thick and glossy. Add 1 teaspoon vanilla. Frost cake while slightly warm.

QUEEN OF NUTS TORTE

SERVES: 12

¼ cup fine fresh bread crumbs
2 ounces almonds
2 ounces pecans
2 ounces walnuts
⅔ cup extra-fine sugar
6 ounces semi-sweet chocolate,
   finely grated
1 Tablespoon butter, softened
1 teaspoon vanilla

finely grated peel of 1
   medium orange
5 eggs, room temperature
   and separated
powdered sugar
fresh orange sections
2 ounces semi-sweet chocolate,
   melted

Butter a 9-inch round cake pan; line bottom with waxed paper cut to fit; butter paper. Sprinkle bread crumbs evenly in pan.

Grind nuts very fine. In a bowl, mix nuts and sugar. Add grated chocolate, butter, vanilla, orange peel and egg yolks. Mix thoroughly.

Beat egg whites until stiff. Stir one-fourth of the whites into the chocolate mixture to lighten batter. Fold in remaining whites. Pour into prepared pan; bake at 350° for 35-45 minutes until quite firm to the touch and cake is beginning to shrink from sides of pan. Cool for 10 minutes in pan; turn out and cool completely.

Store at room temperature tightly wrapped in foil. To serve, dust with powdered sugar and garnish with orange sections partially dipped in melted chocolate.

NOTE: May be prepared 1 or 2 days before serving.

CHOCOLATE CHIP CAKE

SERVES: 12

1 cup boiling water
1 cup chopped dates
1 teaspoon baking soda
1 cup sugar
1 cup margarine
2 eggs
1 teaspoon vanilla

1¾ cups flour
¼ teaspoon salt
1 Tablespoon cocoa
1 cup semi-sweet chocolate
   chips
1 cup chopped pecans

Pour water over dates and soda. Let stand for 5 minutes.

In a mixing bowl, cream sugar and margarine. Add eggs and vanilla.

Combine flour, salt and cocoa. Add dry ingredients to sugar mixture alternately with date mixture. Stir in half of the chocolate chips and half of the nuts. Pour into a well-greased and floured 10-inch tube pan. Sprinkle remaining chocolate chips and nuts on top of the cake. Bake at 350° for 45-50 minutes. Cool in pan for 15 minutes before removing.

CHOCOLATE CREAM PIE

SERVES: 8

"Superb from scratch!"

1 9-inch pastry shell, baked
   (see page 149)
1 cup sugar
3 Tablespoons cornstarch
1¼ ounces unsweetened
   chocolate

½ teaspoon salt
2 cups milk
3 egg yolks
½ teaspoon vanilla
1 cup heavy cream, whipped
semi-sweet chocolate shavings

Prepare pastry shell. Cool.

In a saucepan, combine sugar, cornstarch, chocolate and salt. Stir in milk. Bring to a boil over low heat, stirring constantly; boil for 1 minute.

Remove from heat; quickly beat in egg yolks, one at a time. Return to a boil; cook and stir for 1 minute. Remove from heat; add vanilla. Pour into prepared shell. Chill. To serve, cover with sweetened whipped cream and garnish with chocolate shavings.

CHOCOLATE CHIP PIE

SERVES: 10

1 9-inch pastry shell
   (see page 149)
3 eggs
1½ cups sugar
6 Tablespoons butter, melted
   and cooled
2 teaspoons vanilla

¾ cup flour
1½ cups semi-sweet chocolate
   minichips
1½ cups chopped pecans
vanilla ice cream
semi-sweet chocolate shavings

Prepare pastry shell.

In a mixing bowl, combine eggs, sugar, butter and vanilla, beating until blended. Stir in flour, chocolate chips and pecans; mix well.

Pour filling into pastry shell. Bake at 350° for 1 hour, or until knife inserted in the center comes out clean. Cool pie. Refrigerate for 4 hours or overnight.

To serve, heat pie at 375° for 10 minutes, or until heated through. Serve with vanilla ice cream sprinkled with chocolate shavings.

AUSTRIAN APRICOT TART

SERVES: 8

"A delicate fruit-filled pastry!"

12 ounces dried apricots
1 cup butter, softened
1¼ cups sugar
6 ounces unblanched almonds,
   finely ground
2 egg yolks

1¼ cups flour
⅛ teaspoon salt
1 cup heavy cream
1 Tablespoon powdered sugar
1 teaspoon almond extract

Soak apricots overnight in water to cover.

Cream butter and sugar. Add almonds, yolks, flour and salt. Mix thoroughly. Line one 9-inch tart pan or ten 3-inch diameter tart tins with pastry. Reserve remaining pastry.

Simmer apricots in ¾ cup of soaking water. Stir and break up fruit until water has evaporated. Stir in sugar. Fill pastry.

Roll out reserved dough on lightly floured surface; cut into ¼-inch strips. Make a lattice pattern across tart filling, placing strips ½ inch apart. Bake at 325° for 30 minutes for large tart or 25-30 minutes for small tarts.

Whip cream, adding sugar and extract. Serve tart warm or at room temperature with whipped cream.

DUTCH APPLE PIE
SERVES: 8

"Absolutely super!"

Topping
1 teaspoon cinnamon

⅓ cup sugar

⅓ cup flour

¼ cup butter

Prepare topping by combining all ingredients thoroughly; set aside.

Filling
1 9-inch pastry shell (see below)

¾ cup sugar

2 Tablespoons flour

1 cup sour cream

1 egg

½ teaspoon vanilla

⅛ teaspoon salt

2 cups peeled, cored and chopped tart apples

Prepare pastry shell.

Combine sugar and flour. Add sour cream, egg, vanilla and salt; beat until smooth. Fold in apples. Pour into pastry shell. Bake at 350° for 15 minutes. Reduce heat to 325° and bake for 30 minutes. Remove from oven. Sprinkle topping over pie and return to oven for 20 minutes. Serve warm.

PASTRY
YIELD: 2 10-inch pastry shells or 40 tart shells

"Great for quiches or shells!"

3½ cups flour

¼ teaspoon salt

1 cup butter, chilled

1 egg, slightly beaten

¼ cup vegetable oil

½ cup cold water

In a bowl, combine flour and salt. Cut in butter until mixture resembles oatmeal. In a separate bowl, combine egg, oil and water. Stir liquids into flour mixture. Divide into 2 balls; wrap in plastic wrap. Chill. Roll into desired shells.

For a partially baked shell, prick the bottom and sides well with a fork. Lay a piece of foil over crust and fill with uncooked beans or rice. Bake at 400° for 8-10 minutes. Remove foil and add desired filling. Bake as directed.

For a baked shell, follow above directions, removing foil and beans after 10 minutes. Continue baking until crust is lightly browned.

RUM RAISIN TART WITH WALNUT PASTRY

SERVES: 8

"The greatest!"

Walnut Pastry

1 cup flour
dash salt
1 teaspoon cinnamon
¼ cup finely chopped walnuts
¼ cup sugar

5 Tablespoons cold butter, cut
   into small pieces
1 egg
¼ teaspoon vanilla
1 Tablespoon water

In a bowl, combine flour, salt, cinnamon, walnuts and sugar. Cut in butter with a pastry blender. Combine remaining ingredients. Make a well in the center of the dry ingredients. Pour in liquids. Mix with a fork until dough can be formed into a ball. Wrap in plastic wrap and refrigerate for 1 hour. Roll out on a lightly floured surface. Line a 10-inch tart pan with pastry.

Raisin Filling

½ cup butter, melted
1½ cups sugar
3 eggs, beaten
1 Tablespoon white vinegar
1 teaspoon vanilla

½ teaspoon salt
1 Tablespoon flour
1 cup raisins, plumped in
   ⅓ cup rum
1 cup heavy cream, whipped

In a bowl, combine filling ingredients except cream; mix well. Pour into pastry-lined tart pan. Bake at 350° for 50 minutes. Cool. Serve garnished with sweetened whipped cream.

PÂTE BRISÉE

YIELD: 1 double crust

"Food processor fast!"

2 cups flour
1 teaspoon salt
½ cup butter, cut into
   1-inch pieces

3 Tablespoons margarine
5 Tablespoons ice water

Fit food processor with steel blade; place flour and salt in the bowl. With the motor running, add butter and margarine and process until the mixture is pea sized. With the motor running, add ice water and process until a ball is formed. Wrap in plastic wrap. Chill for 1 hour before rolling.

LEMON MERINGUE PIE

SERVES: 6-8

"Filling is great for tarts, too!"

1 9-inch baked pastry shell
(see page 149)
⅓ cup cornstarch
2 cups sugar
¼ teaspoon salt
1½ cups water

4 eggs, separated
¼ cup fresh lemon juice
2 Tablespoons grated fresh
lemon peel
2 Tablespoons butter
¼ teaspoon cream of tartar

Prepare pastry shell.

In a saucepan, combine cornstarch, 1½ cups sugar and salt. Add water; stir until smooth. Cook over medium heat, stirring constantly. Bring to a boil. Boil for 1 minute.

Remove from heat and beat in 4 egg yolks, one at a time. Return to heat and bring to a boil. Boil for 1 minute. Remove from heat; stir in lemon juice, peel and butter. Pour into shell.

In a bowl, beat 4 egg whites with cream of tartar to soft peaks. Add ½ cup sugar slowly. Beat until stiff. Spread meringue over filling making sure it touches pastry shell. Bake at 400° for 7 minutes or until meringue is lightly browned. Cool.

STRAWBERRY-RHUBARB PIE

SERVES: 8

"Absolutely scrumptious!"

1 9-inch double pastry shell
(see page 149)
1¼ cups sugar
⅛ teaspoon salt

⅓ cup flour
2 cups 1-inch pieces rhubarb
2 cups sliced strawberries
2 Tablespoons butter

Prepare pastry shell.

Combine sugar, salt and flour. Stir in fruit. Spoon mixture into prepared shell. Dot with butter. Top with crust and sprinkle lightly with sugar. Bake at 400° for 40-45 minutes.

APPLE-ALMOND TART

SERVES: 10

Pastry
1 recipe Pâte Brisée
  (see page 150)

Line a 10-inch tart pan with pastry. Chill.

Almond Filling
3 ounces blanched almonds   1 egg
½ cup sugar

In a food processor, grind almonds to a powder; add sugar and egg. Blend to smooth paste; spread over dough. Chill.

Apples
3-4 medium-size tart apples;   3 Tablespoons sugar
  peeled, cored and sliced   2 Tablespoons butter

Arrange sliced apples in overlapping concentric circles on top of filling. Sprinkle with sugar and dot with butter. Bake at 350° for 45-55 minutes. Cool.

Apricot Glaze
6 Tablespoons apricot jam   1 Tablespoon Amaretto
2 Tablespoons sugar

In a small saucepan, combine glaze ingredients and cook until sugar is dissolved; strain. Brush tart with glaze.

FROZEN GRAND MARNIER SOUFFLÉ

SERVES: 6

3 egg yolks, room temperature   1 cup heavy cream
½ (scant) cup sugar   finely grated fresh orange peel
3 Tablespoons Grand Marnier   or lightly toasted almonds

Beat yolks until thick. Gradually add sugar. Beat in Grand Marnier. Whip cream stiff; fold into yolk mixture. Pour into individual small soufflé dishes. Freeze. Serve each soufflé garnished with orange peel or almonds.

GRAND MARNIER SOUFFLÉ

SERVES: 6

"It is divine!"

Soufflé

3 Tablespoons butter, softened
3 Tablespoons sugar
2 Tablespoons flour
½ cup half-and-half
½ cup sugar
4 egg yolks, room temperature

2 teaspoons grated fresh orange
  peel
¼ cup Grand Marnier
5 egg whites, room temperature
¼ teaspoon salt
¼ teaspoon cream of tartar

Using 1 tablespoon of butter, grease an 8-cup soufflé dish. Sprinkle bottom and sides with 2 tablespoons sugar. Turn upside down to remove excess sugar. Preheat oven to 400.°

In a saucepan, melt 2 tablespoons butter. Add flour; cook for 2 minutes. Whisk in half-and-half and ½ cup sugar. Cook until thickened. Remove from heat; quickly beat in the 4 egg yolks, one at a time. Return to heat and cook for 1 minute. Remove from heat; add orange peel and Grand Marnier. Cool slightly.

Beat the 5 egg whites until foamy. Add salt, cream of tartar and 1 tablespoon sugar. Beat until stiff peaks are formed.

Stir one-fourth of whites into yolk mixture. Fold in remaining whites. Pour into prepared soufflé dish. Turn preheated oven down to 375.° Bake for 25-30 minutes. Serve immediately with sauce.

Grand Marnier Sauce

1 egg
2 egg yolks

3 Tablespoons sugar
2 Tablespoons Grand Marnier

In the top of a double boiler, combine egg, yolks, sugar and Grand Marnier. Place over barely simmering water; whisk constantly until mixture thickens. Do not boil. Serve warm.

To make chocolate leaves, select smooth leaves. In a container only large enough to dip a leaf, melt 2 ounces chocolate. Carefully pull the shiny side of a leaf across the chocolate. Remove excess chocolate with a knife point. Refrigerate leaf green-side down for 5-10 minutes. Carefully separate chocolate and green leaves. Chill chocolate leaves.

COLD STRAWBERRY SOUFFLÉ
SERVES: 6-8

3 pints fresh strawberries
2 envelopes unflavored gelatin
1 cup sugar
½ cup water
1 Tablespoon fresh lemon juice

2 Tablespoons Kirsch
3 egg whites
1 cup heavy cream
¼ cup powdered sugar

Collar a 1-quart soufflé dish with a 4-inch strip of oiled foil; fasten foil so it extends 2 inches above top of dish.

Clean berries and reserve ½ pint for garnish. Chop remaining berries.

In a saucepan, mix gelatin and ½ cup sugar; stir in water and cook over low heat until dissolved. Remove from heat; stir in chopped strawberries, lemon juice and Kirsch. Refrigerate; stir occasionally until mixture slightly thickens.

Beat egg whites until soft peaks are formed. Gradually add ½ cup sugar; beat until stiff peaks are formed. Whip ⅔ cup cream. Fold in 3 tablespoons powdered sugar. Fold whites and cream into berry mixture. Pour into prepared mold. Refrigerate for 6 hours.

To serve, whip ⅓ cup cream stiff. Fold in 1 tablespoon powdered sugar. Garnish soufflé with whipped cream rosettes and reserved whole strawberries.

CRÈME ANGLAISE
YIELD: 1¼ cups
"A light custard sauce!"

1 cup whole milk
1 3-inch piece vanilla bean,
  split and pulp removed

3 egg yolks
4½ Tablespoons sugar

In a heavy saucepan, heat milk with vanilla bean and vanilla pulp. Set aside.

In a bowl, combine egg yolks and sugar, whisking until mixture is thick and lemon colored. Gradually whisk milk into egg mixture. Return to saucepan. Place over low heat and cook, stirring constantly, until mixture thickens and coats a spoon. Do not boil. Remove pan from heat; strain custard into a bowl and stir several minutes to cool. Refrigerate until ready to serve.

NOTE: Serve with fresh fruit or Chocolate Charlotte (see page 155).

HOT FUDGE SAUCE

YIELD: 2 cups

"Rich and thick!"

3 ounces unsweetened chocolate ⅓ cup sugar
1 14-ounce can sweetened   ½ cup water
   condensed milk   1 teaspoon vanilla

In the top of a double boiler, melt chocolate over simmering water. Whisk in milk, sugar and water, stirring occasionally until thickened. Remove from heat and stir in vanilla. Serve warm.

CHOCOLATE CHARLOTTE

SERVES: 8

"A creamy mixture in ladyfingers!"

2 packages ladyfingers   4 ounces semi-sweet chocolate
4 eggs, room temperature and   ¼ cup coffee
   separated   ¾ cup unsalted butter, softened
¾ cup sugar   ⅔ cup sugar
¼ cup Grand Marnier

Line bottom of an 8-cup charlotte mold with waxed paper cut to size. Trim one end of 8-10 ladyfingers to a point; arrange in daisy pattern in bottom of mold, rounded side down and pointed end in. Cut small circle from 1 ladyfinger and place in center of daisy. Arrange remaining lady-fingers against sides of mold, rounded side out. Set aside.

In the top of a double boiler, beat 4 egg yolks with ¾ cup sugar until thick and pale yellow in color. Beat in Grand Marnier. Place over simmering water; beat for several minutes until mixture is hot to the touch. Remove from heat; beat for several minutes to cool. Set aside.

Melt chocolate with coffee over low heat. Remove from heat; beat in butter a little at a time. Beat the chocolate mixture into the yolk mixture.

In a large bowl, beat the 4 egg whites until soft peaks are formed. Gradually add ⅔ cup sugar; beat until stiff peaks are formed. Stir one-third of the whites into the chocolate mixture; fold all of the chocolate into the remaining whites. Pour into prepared charlotte mold; refrigerate overnight.

To serve, carefully run a knife around the edge of the mold. Invert onto serving platter and remove mold and paper. Cut charlotte into wedges and serve with Creme Anglaise (see page 154).

NOTE: Chocolate mixture is excellent served separately in dessert dishes with sweetened whipped cream.

BRIE BRÛLÉE
"Something special!"

SERVES: 12

1 8-inch wheel of Brie cheese
1 cup chopped pecans
2 cups brown sugar

Lavosh, mild crisp crackers or
   sliced fresh apples and pears

Remove the top rind from the Brie. Place cheese in a 10-inch quiche dish or pie plate. Sprinkle nuts over top of Brie. Cover top and sides with sugar, patting into place. Broil on lowest oven rack until sugar bubbles and melts, about 3 minutes. Watch carefully to prevent burning. Cheese should retain its shape. Serve immediately with crackers or fruit.

NOTE: May be prepared ahead to broiling point, covered and refrigerated. Return to room temperature before broiling.

BAKED PINEAPPLE

SERVES: 4

2 medium-size fresh pineapples
sugar

2-3 Tablespoons rum
¼ cup butter

Slice pineapples in half lengthwise including tops. Carefully carve out inside; cut into bite-size pieces. In a bowl, sweeten pineapple to taste with sugar; flavor with rum. Return pineapple to shells; dot with butter. Cover with foil (including green leaves). Place on baking sheet and bake at 350° for 30 minutes. Serve warm. May be served plain or with Natillas Sauce (see below).

NATILLAS
"Ole! Spanish vanilla sauce!"

YIELD: 2¼ cups

¼ cup sugar
1 teaspoon cornstarch
¼ teaspoon salt
1 egg

2 egg yolks
2 cups half-and-half
1 teaspoon vanilla

In the top of a double boiler, combine sugar, cornstarch, salt, egg and yolks; mix well. Add half-and-half. Whisk over simmering water until slightly thickened. Remove from heat; add vanilla. Chill.

NOTE: Marvelous over red berries in season or Baked Pineapple (see above).

LEMON MOUSSE WITH STRAWBERRY SAUCE

SERVES: 8

"Light and refreshing!"

Mousse

1 envelope unflavored gelatin
¼ cup cold water
4 eggs, room temperature and
  separated
¼ teaspoon salt
½ cup fresh lemon juice

1¼ cups sugar
1 teaspoon grated fresh lemon
  peel
1 cup heavy cream, whipped
⅓ cup powdered sugar

Sprinkle gelatin over cold water to soften.

In the top of a double boiler, whisk egg yolks with salt, lemon juice and ½ cup sugar. Cook over simmering water; stir constantly until slightly thickened. Remove from heat; stir in lemon peel and gelatin mixture. Cool.

Whip cream until stiff; sweeten with powdered sugar. Set aside.

In a large bowl, beat egg whites until soft peaks are formed. Add ¾ cup sugar; gradually beat until stiff peaks are formed. Fold lemon mixture and whipped cream into whites. Pour into a glass serving bowl or individual serving dishes. Refrigerate for 5 hours. Serve with Strawberry Sauce.

Strawberry Sauce

4 cups sliced fresh strawberries
¾ cup sugar
½ cup currant jelly

2 Tablespoons Grand Marnier
¼ cup Kirsch

In a blender or food processor, puree berries and sugar. Pass mixture through a fine sieve. Set aside.

In a small saucepan, heat jelly, Grand Marnier and Kirsch until jelly is completely dissolved. Stir in strawberry puree. Chill before serving.

CHOCOLATE FONDUE

SERVES: 4

3 Tablespoons heavy cream
6 ounces sweet chocolate
pinch of cinnamon

1 Tablespoon brandy
fresh fruits or pound cake
  for dipping

In a saucepan, warm cream over low heat. Break chocolate into small pieces and add to cream, stirring to make a smooth sauce. Stir in cinnamon and brandy. Serve warm with fresh fruits or pieces of pound cake.

NOTE: During the holiday season, substitute egg nog for the heavy cream.

DESSERTS

CHOCOLATE MOUSSE DIVINE

SERVES: 12

"Sinfully delicious!"

1½ cups chopped pecans
3 Tablespoons brown sugar
3 Tablespoons butter, melted
2 teaspoons rum
8 ounces semi-sweet chocolate

1 egg
2 eggs, room temperature
  and separated
2 cups heavy cream
⅓ cup powdered sugar

Combine pecans, brown sugar, butter and rum. Press into the bottom of an 8-inch or 9-inch springform pan. Chill while preparing filling.

In a double boiler, melt chocolate. Cool slightly. Whisk in the whole egg and the 2 egg yolks.

Beat 2 egg whites until stiff; stir a small amount of whites into chocolate mixture to lighten. Fold in remaining whites.

Beat 1 cup cream until stiff; add powdered sugar. Fold into chocolate mixture. Pour onto prepared crust; refrigerate for 6-8 hours.

To serve, whip 1 cup cream and sweeten to taste. Decorate mousse with whipped cream rosettes and chocolate leaves (see page 153).

CHOCOLATE KAHLUA MOUSSE

SERVES: 12

"An elegant dessert!"

2 dozen almond or coconut
  macaroons
Kahlua
1 4-ounce package ladyfingers
12 eggs, room temperature
  and separated

1½ cups butter, softened
1½ cups powdered sugar
12 ounces German's Sweet
  Chocolate, melted
1 cup heavy cream

Soak macaroons in Kahlua until saturated; gently squeeze out excess moisture. Press macaroons, slightly overlapping, into the bottom of a 10-inch, lightly oiled springform tube pan. Line sides of pan with split ladyfingers, cut side in.

Beat egg whites until stiff. Set aside.

In a large bowl, beat egg yolks with butter. Add powdered sugar and chocolate. Fold in egg whites. Pour into pan. Refrigerate ovenight. Unmold and serve with Kahlua-flavored, slightly sweetened whipped cream.

NOTE: May be frozen.

WHITE CHOCOLATE MOUSSE
"Worth the cost!"

SERVES: 6-8

1 vanilla bean
½ cup powdered sugar, sifted
6 ounces white chocolate,
  coarsely chopped
6 Tablespoons butter, room
  temperature
4 eggs, room temperature and
  separated

1 cup heavy cream
pinch of cream of tartar
2 ounces semi-sweet or
  bittersweet chocolate
3 Tablespoons shelled, chopped
  pistachio nuts

Remove pulp from vanilla bean. Combine pulp with powdered sugar; set aside.

In a saucepan, melt white chocolate with 4 tablespoons butter over lowest heat; stir until smooth.

In a heavy saucepan, beat egg yolks with powdered sugar until pale yellow. Whisk over low heat for several minutes until warm. Remove from heat. Whisk in melted white chocolate; continue beating until tepid.

Beat cream until stiff; set aside.

Beat egg whites until foamy. Add cream of tartar; continue beating until stiff but not dry. Stir one-fourth of beaten whites into white chocolate mixture to lighten; gently fold in remainder of whites. Fold in whipped cream. Spoon mousse into goblets; cover and refrigerate. One and one-half hours before serving, place goblets in freezer. At serving time, melt dark chocolate with 2 tablespoons butter. Drizzle sauce over each serving; sprinkle with nuts.

ELEGANT STRAWBERRIES
"An impressive dessert!"

SERVES: 6

¾ cup sugar
½ cup heavy cream
¼ cup light corn syrup
2 Tablespoons butter

½ cup chopped Heath Toffee
  candy bars
1 quart fresh strawberries,
  washed and hulled
1 cup sour cream

In a saucepan, combine sugar, cream, corn syrup and butter. Bring to a boil and cook for 3 minutes. Stir occasionally to prevent boiling over. Remove from heat and add candy. Stir until most of the candy is dissolved. Cool. Serve strawberries topped with a dollop of sour cream; drizzle with sauce.

COOKING CLUB ORANGES
SERVES: 8

"Delectable!"

8-10 small navel oranges
½ cup butter
grated peel of 1 medium lemon
⅓ cup fresh lemon juice
¼ teaspoon salt
1¾ cups sugar

3 eggs, room temperature
 and separated
1 cup heavy cream
1 teaspoon cream of tartar
fresh mint leaves

Remove a 1-inch slice from the top of each orange; scoop out and discard pulp. Place shells in freezer.

In the top of a double boiler, whisk butter, lemon peel, lemon juice, salt, 1½ cups sugar and egg yolks. Place over simmering water. Cook, stirring until shiny and thick; cool.

Whip cream until stiff; fold into lemon mixture. Cover and freeze for at least 4 hours.

Before serving, beat egg whites with a pinch of salt and cream of tartar until soft peaks are formed. Gradually add ¼ cup sugar; beat until glossy and stiff.

To serve, fill orange shells two-thirds full with lemon mousse. Pipe or spread meringue on top. Place 6 inches from a preheated broiler until lightly browned, about 15-25 seconds. Watch carefully. Garnish with fresh mint leaves; serve immediately.

HOMEMADE CHOCOLATE ICE CREAM
YIELD: 2½ quarts

"For choco-holics!"

5⅓ cups heavy cream
2⅔ cups whole milk
¾ cup Droste cocoa
1 cup finely grated semi-sweet
 chocolate

⅛ teaspoon salt
1 vanilla bean, split and
 pulp removed
12 egg yolks
3 cups extra-fine sugar

In a large saucepan, heat cream and milk. Add cocoa, chocolate, salt and vanilla pulp; stir until chocolate is melted.

In a mixing bowl, beat yolks. Gradually add sugar. Stirring constantly, slowly strain some of the chocolate mixture into the yolks. Blend in remaining chocolate. Return mixture to saucepan. Cook over low heat until mixture lightly coats a spoon. Do not boil. Refrigerate mixture until thoroughly chilled. Freeze slowly according to ice cream freezer directions.

CINNAMON CHOCOLATE TORTE

SERVES: 16

"Looks impressive!"

2¾ cups sifted flour
2 Tablespoons cinnamon
1½ cups butter
2 cups sugar
2 eggs
4 cups heavy cream

1 Tablespoon vanilla
½ cup powdered sugar
1 ounce unsweetened chocolate,
   finely grated
2 ounces semi-sweet chocolate,
   curled

Cut twelve 9-inch circles of waxed paper. Grease two 9-inch round cake pans. Line each cake pan with a waxed paper circle; grease.

Sift flour with cinnamon; set aside.

In a mixing bowl, cream butter with sugar. Add eggs; beat well. Add flour mixture, a little at a time. Spread ⅓ cup batter in a very thin layer in each cake pan. Bake at 375° for 8 minutes or until edges are slightly brown. Cool for 5 minutes. Carefully remove torte layer from pan; remove paper. Repeat with remaining batter to make 12 torte layers.

Whip cream until soft peaks are formed. Add vanilla and powdered sugar. Beat until stiff peaks are formed.

Arrange one torte layer on a flat platter. Spread with ⅓ cup whipped cream. Repeat layering torte and cream, ending with cream. Fold unsweetened chocolate into remaining whipped cream. Mound on top of torte. Decorate with chocolate curls. Refrigerate for 2-3 hours before serving.

STRAWBERRIES IN SHERRY CREAM

SERVES: 8

5 egg yolks
1 cup sugar
½ cup dry sherry

1 cup heavy cream, whipped
1 quart fresh strawberries,
   hulled and halved

In the top of a double boiler, place egg yolks. Beat until thick and lemon colored. Beat in sugar; add sherry. Place over simmering water, beating until thick. Cool. At serving time, fold in whipped cream and strawberries. Serve in champagne glasses.

NOTE: Sherry cream, without the strawberries, is delicious over other fruits or pound cake.

PETITE FLOATING ISLANDS
SERVES: 6-8

"Enjoyed by all!"

Custard

6 egg yolks
¾ cup sugar
1 vanilla bean, split and
   pulp removed

1 Tablespoon cornstarch
3 cups whole milk

In a saucepan, combine yolks, sugar, vanilla pulp and cornstarch. Whisk in milk. Cook over low heat; stir constantly until sauce thickens. Do not boil. Strain into a bowl. Stir sauce occasionally as it cools.

Meringue

3 egg whites, room temperature
½ cup powdered sugar

3 cups whole milk

Beat egg whites until soft peaks are formed. Add sugar slowly; continue to beat for 1 minute.

In a large shallow pan, bring milk to a simmer. Drop meringue by spoonfuls into milk. Cook for 2 minutes on each side; do not over cook. Remove meringues from milk with a slotted spoon; place on paper towels. To serve, place a portion of custard into an individual serving bowl; top with an "island."

COFFEE TORTONI
SERVES: 6

2 Tablespoons flaked coconut
2 Tablespoons finely chopped
   almonds
1 egg white
1 Tablespoon dry instant coffee

6 Tablespoons sugar
1 cup heavy cream
1 teaspoon vanilla
⅛ teaspoon almond extract

Place coconut and almonds in an 8-inch cake pan. Broil for a few seconds to toast lightly.

Whip egg white and coffee, gradually adding 2 tablespoons sugar. Pour cream into this mixture and whip. Gradually add 4 tablespoons of sugar and extracts. Whip until firm but not stiff.

Fold half of the almonds and coconut into coffee mixture. Spoon into small, elegant serving dishes. Top with remaining almond-coconut mixture. Freeze until firm, about 2-3 hours or overnight. Remove from freezer 15 minutes before serving.

APPLE CREPES

SERVES: 6-8

Crepes

2 eggs
½ cup milk
½ cup water
2 Tablespoons sugar

1 Tablespoon apple brandy
1 Tablespoon butter, melted
1 cup flour
3 Tablespoons unsalted butter

In a blender, combine eggs, milk, water, sugar, brandy and melted butter. Add flour; blend on high speed for 1 minute, scraping down any flour particles that adhere to sides of the blender. Refrigerate for 2 hours.

To cook crepes, heat an 8-inch skillet; brush with unsalted butter. Add enough batter to just coat the bottom. Cook until underside is lightly browned; turn crepe over and brown other side. Repeat process. Crepes may be prepared ahead and stacked between sheets of waxed paper. Store in refrigerator or freezer.

Apple Filling

10 Tablespoons unsalted butter
8 medium-size tart apples;
  peeled, cored and cut into
  ½-inch slices

1 cup sugar

In a large skillet, melt butter. Add apples and sugar. Cook apples slowly, turning occasionally until well caramelized, about 10-12 minutes. If needed, thicken juices with a small amount of cornstarch.

Butter Mixture

6 Tablespoons unsalted butter,
  softened
⅓ cup sugar

2 Tablespoons apple juice
2 Tablespoons apple brandy

Cream butter and sugar. Blend in apple juice and brandy.

To assemble crepes, spread ½ teaspoon butter mixture on light side of crepe. Spoon 3 tablespoons apple mixture over lower third of each crepe; roll up. Place crepes in a greased baking dish seam-side down. Spread with remaining butter mixture. Cover and bake at 375° for 10-15 minutes. To serve, flame with 3 tablespoons apple brandy or serve with Crème Anglaise (see page 154).

To make extra-fine sugar, place sugar in a food processor bowl fitted with a steel blade. Cover bowl with plastic wrap and secure lid. Process 2-3 minutes.

POACHED PEARS   SERVES: 6

6 firm pears
1 bottle Cabernet Sauvignon
1¼ cups sugar
2 whole cloves

1 3-inch stick of cinnamon
2 orange slices
2 lemon slices
¾ cup heavy cream, whipped

Peel pears leaving stems attached; core bottom and remove seeds. Place in acidulated water to keep from discoloring.

In a kettle only large enough to hold the pears, bring wine, sugar, cloves, cinnamon and sliced fruits to a boil. Remove pears from water and place in syrup. Cover and cook for 8 minutes or until tender. Cool in poaching syrup overnight. Remove pears from liquid. Garnish with slightly sweetened whipped cream and a green leaf placed next to the stem.

NOTE: Pears are delicious served with plain Sherry Cream (see page 161).

SPRING RHUBARB COBBLER   SERVES: 9

Rhubarb Filling
2 cups sugar
¼ cup cornstarch
½ teaspoon cinnamon
¼ teaspoon nutmeg

¾ cup water
2 pounds rhubarb, cut into
  1-inch pieces
2 Tablespoons butter

In a saucepan, combine sugar, cornstarch, cinnamon, nutmeg and water. Add rhubarb. Cook and stir until boiling. Boil for 2 minutes. Pour into a 9-inch square baking dish; dot with butter. Place in a 400° oven. Immediately prepare biscuits.

Orange-Pecan Biscuits
1 cup sifted flour
⅓ cup sugar
1½ teaspoons baking powder
½ teaspoon salt
¼ cup butter

⅓ cup milk
¼ cup chopped pecans
1 teaspoon grated fresh orange
  peel

Sift dry ingredients. Cut in butter. Stir in milk, pecans and orange peel. Drop by spoonfuls atop hot rhubarb mixture. Bake at 400° for 15 minutes.

PAVLOVA
SERVES: 10
"A dramatic finale!"

Pavlova
4 egg whites, room temperature — ½ teaspoon vanilla
1 cup sugar — 1 Tablespoon cornstarch
1 teaspoon white vinegar

Preheat oven to 400°. Line baking sheet with aluminum foil. Lightly butter foil.

In a bowl, beat egg whites until stiff but not dry. Add sugar gradually, beating constantly. Add vinegar and vanilla; beat for 5 minutes. Add cornstarch; beat for 1 minute.

Mound meringue onto prepared baking sheet into a disc about 2 inches high. Imprint edge of disc with the back of a spoon with an upward motion. Place in oven; reduce heat to 250°. Bake for 1½ hours. Cool.

Topping
1 cup heavy cream — 1 pint fresh fruit
⅓ cup powdered sugar

Beat cream until soft peaks are formed. Gradually add sugar, beating until stiff peaks are formed. Fold in fruit. Mound fruited cream in center of Pavlova. Cut into wedges to serve.

CARAMEL CORN
YIELD: 5 quarts
"Everyone loves it!"

2 cups brown sugar — ⅛ teaspoon cream of tartar
½ cup light corn syrup — dash of salt
1 cup margarine — 5 quarts popped corn
1 teaspoon baking soda

In a heavy saucepan, mix sugar, syrup and margarine. Bring to a boil and cook for 5 minutes, stirring occasionally. Remove from heat and add soda, cream of tartar and salt. Immediately pour over corn; mix thoroughly. Place in a large roasting pan and bake at 200° for 1 hour. Turn onto waxed paper. Cool. Break into pieces.

GOLDEN CARAMELS
YIELD: 3 dozen
"Children could make these!"

1 cup sugar
½ cup brown sugar
½ cup light corn syrup

1½ cups heavy cream
¼ cup butter
1 teaspoon vanilla

In a saucepan, combine all ingredients except vanilla. Cook and stir over medium heat until mixture boils. Continue cooking, stirring occasionally, to firm ball state (248°), 30-45 minutes. Remove from heat; stir in vanilla. Pour into a buttered 8-inch square pan. Cool. Cut and wrap in waxed paper.

ROYAL MARBLE CHEESECAKE
SERVES: 12
"Smooth!"

¾ cup flour
2 Tablespoons sugar
¼ teaspoon salt
¼ cup butter, melted
1 cup semi-sweet chocolate chips, melted

3 8-ounce packages cream cheese, softened
1¼ cups sugar
4 eggs
2 teaspoons vanilla
1 cup sour cream

Combine flour, 2 tablespoons sugar, salt, butter and 2 tablespoons of the melted chocolate. Press into the bottom of a 9-inch springform pan. Bake at 350° for 5 minutes.

In a mixing bowl, beat cream cheese, 1¼ cups sugar, eggs, vanilla and sour cream. Remove 1½ cups of the cheese mixture; stir into melted chocolate.

Pour half of the remaining cheese mixture onto the crust; top with spoonfuls of half the chocolate mixture. Cover with remaining cheese mixture and top with remaining spoonfuls of the chocolate mixture. Cut through the batter with a knife to marble. Bake at 350° for 50-55 minutes. Cool and chill.

Bain marie is a pan containing hot water into which another pan is placed for baking.

DANISH CREAM

SERVES: 6

"Easy and elegant!"

1 cup heavy cream
1 cup sugar
1¼ teaspoons unflavored gelatin
1 cup sour cream

½ teaspoon vanilla
1 10-ounce package frozen
   raspberries, thawed

In a saucepan, combine heavy cream, sugar and gelatin. Heat gently until gelatin and sugar are dissolved. Remove from heat; cool until slightly thickened, about 10 minutes.

Stir in sour cream and vanilla. Spoon into individual bowls; chill. Serve topped with raspberries.

PRALINE CHEESECAKE

SERVES: 12

Cheesecake

¾ cup graham cracker crumbs
2 Tablespoons sugar
¼ cup chopped pecans
3 Tablespoons butter, melted
3 8-ounce packages cream
   cheese, softened
1 cup brown sugar

1 5½-ounce can evaporated
   milk
2 Tablespoons flour
1½ teaspoons vanilla
3 eggs
12 pecan halves for garnish

Combine cracker crumbs, sugar, chopped pecans and butter. Press onto the bottom of a 9-inch springform pan. Bake at 350° for 5 minutes.

Beat cream cheese, brown sugar, milk, flour and vanilla. Add eggs, one at a time; beat well after each addition. Pour onto baked crust. Bake at 350° for 45-50 minutes. Garnish with pecan halves; chill.

Praline Sauce

1 cup dark corn syrup
2 Tablespoons cornstarch

2 Tablespoons brown sugar
1 teaspoon vanilla

In a heavy saucepan, combine corn syrup, cornstarch and brown sugar. Cook, stirring until thickened. Remove from heat; stir in vanilla. Cool slightly. Serve cheesecake with sauce.

CHOCOLATE SWIRL CHEESECAKE

SERVES: 12

Crust
1 cup chocolate wafer crumbs | 3 Tablespoons butter, melted

Thoroughly combine wafer crumbs and butter. Press evenly on the bottom of a 9-inch or 10-inch springform pan. Bake at 350° for 5 minutes.

Cheesecake
3 8-ounce packages cream
  cheese, softened
1⅓ cups sugar
3 eggs

2 teaspoons vanilla
3 ounces semi-sweet chocolate,
  melted

In a mixing bowl, beat cream cheese and sugar. Add eggs and vanilla; beat until smooth. Pour mixture onto prepared crust. Drizzle melted chocolate on cheesecake and swirl with a knife. Bake at 350° for 50 minutes.

Topping
1½ cups sour cream
¼ cup sugar

1 teaspoon vanilla

Thoroughly mix topping ingredients. Pour onto cheesecake. Bake at 350° for 5 minutes. Cool and chill.

SNOW ICE CREAM

SERVES: 8

"For wintry days!"

2 cups heavy cream
1½ cups sifted powdered sugar
1½ Tablespoons vanilla

⅛ teaspoon almond extract
large bowl of fresh snow

In a chilled bowl, combine cream, sugar and extracts. Gradually whisk in some of the snow until mixture is thick and well combined. If too thin, add more snow. If too thick, add more cream. Adjust flavor by adding sugar or vanilla. Store in freezer. Serve plain or with chocolate sauce.

To prevent raisins from sinking to the bottom of quick breads, puddings and desserts, soak raisins in a small quantity of liquid. Drain before adding to mixture.

APPLE DUMPLINGS

SERVES: 6

"You're gonna love 'em!"

Filling
½ cup sugar   1 Tablespoon butter, softened
½ teaspoon cinnamon

Combine all ingredients; set aside.

Syrup
1½ cups sugar   3 Tablespoons butter
1 teaspoon cinnamon   1½ cups water

In a saucepan, combine syrup ingredients and boil for 3 minutes; set aside.

Pastry
3 cups flour   ½ cup margarine
1 teaspoon salt   10 Tablespoons ice water
½ cup shortening

Combine flour and salt. Cut in shortening and margarine to small pea sized.
Add enough ice water to form a pastry dough.

Divide pastry into 6 equal portions. Wrap and refrigerate if not used
immediately.

6 medium-size, tart cooking   1½ cups heavy cream
   apples

Peel and core apples. Roll pastry into a circle ⅛ inch thick. Place apple in
center of dough. Pack cavity with 1 tablespoon of filling mixture. Wrap
dough up and over apple to enclose completely. Insert wooden picks to
secure. Repeat for remaining apples. Place in a 9 x 13-inch baking pan.
Bake at 350° for 30 minutes. Pour syrup over tops of dumplings and bake
for 30 minutes. Serve warm with cream.

STRAWBERRIES IN WHITE CHOCOLATE

SERVES: 8

"A sweet delicacy!"

1 quart fresh, whole   6 ounces Tobler Narcisse
   strawberries   white chocolate
1 Tablespoon shortening

Wash strawberries; dry thoroughly.

Over very low heat, melt shortening with chocolate. When chocolate is
smooth, dip three-fourths of each berry into chocolate, holding by stem.
Place on waxed paper; chill until serving time.

SCRUMPTIOUS ICE CREAM TORTE SERVES: 16

8 ounces semi-sweet chocolate
1 cup heavy cream
½ teaspoon dry instant coffee
1 Tablespoon brandy
1 8½-ounce package chocolate
  wafers, crushed

1 quart chocolate ice cream,
  softened
1 quart vanilla ice cream,
  softened
4 ounces English toffee candy,
  coarsely chopped

In a saucepan, melt chocolate with cream and coffee over low heat, stirring until smooth. Remove from heat; stir in brandy. Set aside.

Grease the bottom of a 9-inch springform pan. Place half the wafer crumbs on the bottom. Spread chocolate ice cream carefully on top of crumbs. Drizzle one-third of the chocolate sauce over the ice cream. Sprinkle remaining crumbs over sauce. Spread vanilla ice cream and drizzle one-third of the chocolate sauce on top. Reserve one-third of the sauce to serve with torte. Sprinkle candy over top. Place torte in freezer until firm. To serve, remove springform sides of pan about 5 minutes before serving. Warm reserved sauce and serve with torte.

STEAMED CHOCOLATE PUDDING SERVES: 8
"A holiday tradition!"

Pudding
¾ cup powdered sugar
1 Tablespoon butter
1 egg
1¼ cups flour

½ cup milk, warmed
2 ounces unsweetened chocolate
2 teaspoons baking powder

In a mixing bowl, beat all ingredients. Place in a buttered steamer; cover. Place steamer in a pan of simmering water. Water should come halfway up sides of the steamer. Cook for 45 minutes. Add more water as needed. Remove mold from water; cool for 15 minutes. Unmold; serve warm with Gorgeous Sauce.

Gorgeous Sauce
½ cup sugar
½ cup heavy cream
¼ cup butter

In the top of a double boiler, combine sauce ingredients. Place over simmering water; cook for 15 minutes, stirring occasionally. Serve warm.

RICE PUDDING

1 cup rice
1 cup water
1 quart whole milk
¼ cup butter
3 eggs

1 cup golden raisins
1 teaspoon vanilla
¾ cup sugar
2 Tablespoons sugar
1 teaspoon cinnamon

Pour rice into rapidly boiling, lightly salted water. Cover and cook for 7 minutes. All water should be absorbed, and the rice will be al denté. Add the milk and butter. Stir gently until butter melts. Bring to a boil. Cover and cook slowly over low heat for 1 hour.

While the rice is cooking, beat the eggs; stir in raisins and vanilla. Set aside.

When the rice is done, stir in ¾ cup sugar. Off the heat, quickly add the egg-raisin mixture. Return rice to heat, stirring until mixture begins to thicken. Do not boil. Pour into a glass serving bowl. Combine 2 tablespoons of sugar with the cinnamon. Sprinkle over pudding. Serve warm or chilled.

FLAN
SERVES: 8
"A Mexican dessert!"

1¾ cups sugar
¼ cup water
6 eggs

⅛ teaspoon salt
1 teaspoon vanilla
1 quart half-and-half

In a saucepan, combine 1 cup sugar and water. Swirl pan over moderately high heat until sugar has dissolved. Allow mixture to boil; swirl pan occasionally until syrup turns a light brown. Do not let sugar over-caramelize as bitter taste will result. Immediately pour caramel into large mold or spoon into individual molds. Caramel will harden rapidly as it cools but melt when baked.

In a mixing bowl, beat eggs. Add ¾ cup sugar, salt, vanilla and half-and-half. Pour into prepared mold. Place in a bain marie (see page 166). Bake at 350° for 45 minutes or until a knife inserted in the center comes out clean. Chill. To serve, run a knife around edge of mold; invert onto serving platter.

PÊCHES AU VIN
SERVES: 6

"A light summer dessert!"

juice of 1 lemon
½ cup sugar

6 medium-size fresh peaches,
  peeled and sliced
1 bottle dry white wine

In a bowl, combine lemon juice and sugar. Stir in peaches. Add just enough wine to cover peaches. Place plastic wrap on surface and refrigerate for at least 3 hours. Serve peaches with juice in chilled champagne glasses with Rolled Sugar Cookies (see page 137) or Meltaways (see page 138).

INDIVIDUAL MERINGUES
YIELD: 1½ dozen

"Fill with ice cream, custard or fruit!"

5 egg whites, room temperature
¼ teaspoon cream of tartar
1½ cups extra-fine sugar

¼ teaspoon almond extract or
½ teaspoon vanilla

In a mixing bowl, beat egg whites until frothy. Add cream of tartar. Beat until soft peaks are formed. Continue beating, gradually adding the sugar. Beat whites until stiff but not dry. Form shells 3 inches in diameter on baking sheets covered with brown paper or foil. Bake at 250° for 55 minutes. Turn off oven and allow to cool in oven with the door closed for 3 hours.

HEAVENLY CHOCOLATE SAUCE
YIELD: 3 cups

"Delicious hot or cold!"

½ cup butter
2 ounces unsweetened chocolate
3 cups sugar

1 13-ounce can evaporated milk
1 teaspoon vanilla

In the top of a double boiler, place butter and chocolate. Place top over simmering water, stirring as chocolate and butter melt. Add sugar. Stir in milk and cook until thickened and smooth, about 15-20 minutes. Remove from heat and add vanilla.

MENUS AND PICKS

In 1893, KATHERINE LEE BATES, an English instructor
at Wellesley College, came to teach a summer session at
Colorado College (another young professor, Woodrow
Wilson, was also lecturing at Colorado College that
summer—in political history!). Bates' account of her
summer in the Rockies is a glorious description of trips to
such places as Manitou, Cripple Creek and various lakes
and canyons with ". . . bluffs and cascades innumerable."
On July 22, she went with friends to Cascade by train.
From there they ascended to the top of Pikes Peak in a
wagon pulled part way by horses and the remainder of the
way by mules. She recorded in her journal that this
was the "most glorious scenery I ever beheld." Katherine
had traveled in the most famous mountains in Europe, yet
she was so moved by the beauty of the Colorado mountains
that she was inspired to write her famous poem,
"America the Beautiful." The first few lines sprang into
her head as she gazed upon the spectacular view from
the top of Pikes Peak. She wrote the remainder of the
poem upon returning to Colorado Springs that evening.

MENUS

Elegant Dinner Parties

Beef Tenderloin with Sauce Claret.....pg. 78

Garden Stuffed Tomatoes.....pg. 107

Rice and Vermicelli.....pg. 129

Salad Vinaigrette

White Chocolate Mousse.....pg. 159

or

Chocolate Kahlua Mousse.....pg. 158

❧

Steak Diane.....pg. 75

or

Steak au Poivre.....pg. 69

Carrots and Leeks Julienne.....pg. 109

Camembert Soufflé.....pg. 121

Garden of the Gods Salad.....pg. 38

Pavlova.....pg. 165

A Sports Night Supper

Bean and Sausage Soup.....pg. 23

Swedish Rye Bread.....pg. 57

Mixed Greens with Creamy Garlic Salad Dressing.....pg. 44

Royal Marble Cheesecake.....pg. 166

Casual Dinner Parties

English Beef. . . . . pg. 69

Yorkshire Pudding. . . . . pg. 117

French Peas. . . . . pg. 112

Chateau Salad. . . . . pg. 38

Apple Dumplings. . . . . pg. 169

or

Dutch Apple Pie. . . . . pg. 149

❧

Mushroom Paté. . . . . pg. 14

Chicken Curry with Condiments. . . . . pg. 82

Steamed Rice

Danish Cream. . . . . pg. 167

Children's Party

Barbecued Beef on Buns. . . . . pg. 81

French Fries

Homemade Chocolate Ice Cream. . . . . pg. 160

Rolled Sugar Cookies. . . . . pg. 137

Family Fare

Italian Meatloaf Whirl.....pg. 80

Fresh Green Vegetable

Egg Noodles.....pg. 127

Deluxe Chocolate Cake.....pg. 141

❧

Italian Meat Balls.....pg. 76

Spaghetti with Italian Red Sauce.....pg. 76

Pita Bread Wedges.....pg. 64

Mixed Greens with Italian Vinaigrette.....pg. 31

Coffee Tortoni.....pg. 162

Autumn Brunch

Orange Ambrosia.....pg. 29

Eggs of Your Choice

Escalloped Bacon.....pg. 93

Cinnamon Rolls.....pg. 64

Aspen Gold Picnic

Seafood Quiche. . . . . pg. 122

Green Grapes Elegant. . . . . pg. 29

Strike-It-Rich Bars. . . . . pg. 131

Après-ski

Hot Buttered Rum. . . . . pg. 17

Salmon Cheese Canapes. . . . . pg. 10

Skier Stew with Dumplings. . . . . pg. 77

Spinach Salad. . . . . pg. 37

Three-Layer Brownies. . . . . pg. 134

❦

Hot Spiced Wine. . . . . pg. 18

Italian Sausage Soup. . . . . pg. 19

Pork 'n' Greens. . . . . pg. 42

Cold-Oven Popovers. . . . . pg. 65

Snow Ice Cream. . . . . pg. 168

Heavenly Chocolate Sauce. . . . . pg. 172

After—the Theater Supper

Gourmet Open-Faced Sandwich.....pg. 102

or

The Goldminer.....pg. 103

Chocolate Charlotte with Crème Anglaise.....pg. 155

Luncheon in the Rockies

Mint Tea.....pg. 17

Summer Salad with Raspberry Mayonnaise.....pg. 40

or

Shrimp-Stuffed Artichokes.....pg. 43

Super Refrigerator Crescents.....pg. 59

Petite Cooking Club Oranges.....pg. 160

or

Elegant Strawberries.....pg. 159

Southwestern Cocktail Party

Magnificent Margaritas.....pg. 18

Sangria.....pg. 17

Tex-Mex Dip.....pg. 8

Tortilla Pinwheels.....pg. 7

Chili Con Queso.....pg. 9

Toasted Butter Pecans.....pg. 11

PICKS

The PICK identifies those recipes in which total preparation time is no more than 15 minutes. Freezing or chilling may be needed beyond that time, but your attention will not be required. The following list is a quick reference of the PICK recipes.

APPETIZERS
Chili Dip 10
Curry Canape 15
Curry Dip 14
Guacamole 11
Hot Spiced Wine 18
Liptauer Cheese 16
Magnificent Margaritas 18
Mozzarella Vegetable Dip 12
Polynesian Ginger Dip 7
Sangria 17
Sour Cream Fruit Dip 9
Vegetable Garden Dip 9

SOUPS
Cold Avocado Soup 26
Creamy Chicken and Green Vegetable Soup 22

SALADS
Belvedere Salad Dressing 45
Celery Seed Dressing 46
Creamy Garlic Salad Dressing 44
Creamy Honey Dressing 44
Fruit Salad Dressing 46
Green Grapes Elegant 29
Lima Beans and Water Chestnuts 33
Mayonnaise 45
Mint Dressing 46
Orange Ambrosia 29
Orange Vinaigrette Salad Dressing 45

BREADS
Applesauce Muffins 51
Creamy Honey Butter 63
Pita Bread Cheese Wedges 64
Yogurt Pancakes 53

NOTES:

INDEX

185

COOKBOOK ORDER FORM

NUGGETS
The Junior League of Colorado Springs, Inc.
P.O. Box 1058, Colorado Springs, CO 80901

Please send me _____ copies of **NUGGETS**

	@	$ 13.95 each	$_____
Add postage and handling	@	$ 1.75 each	$_____
If desired, add gift wrap	@	$ .50 each	$_____
Add sales tax for delivery in Colorado	@	$ .77 each	$_____
Please furnish gift enclosure card	@	$ .25 each	$_____
TOTAL ENCLOSED			$_____

Make checks payable to **NUGGETS**

☐ Visa ⬜⬜⬜⬜⬜⬜⬜⬜⬜⬜⬜⬜⬜⬜⬜⬜⬜

☐ MasterCard ⬜⬜⬜⬜⬜⬜⬜⬜⬜⬜⬜⬜⬜⬜⬜⬜

Signature _____ Expiration Date _____

Name _____

Address _____

City _____ State _____ Zip _____

MAILING LABEL – PLEASE PRINT

FROM: Junior League of Colorado Springs, Inc.
P.O. Box 1058, Colorado Springs, CO 80901

TO: Name _____

Address _____

City _____

State _____ Zip _____

COOKBOOK ORDER FORM

NUGGETS
The Junior League of Colorado Springs, Inc.
P.O. Box 1058, Colorado Springs, CO 80901

Please send me _____ copies of **NUGGETS**

	@	$ 13.95 each	$_____
Add postage and handling	@	$ 1.75 each	$_____
If desired, add gift wrap	@	$ .50 each	$_____
Add sales tax for delivery in Colorado	@	$ .77 each	$_____
Please furnish gift enclosure card	@	$ .25 each	$_____
TOTAL ENCLOSED			$_____

Make checks payable to **NUGGETS**

☐ Visa ⬜⬜⬜⬜⬜⬜⬜⬜⬜⬜⬜⬜⬜⬜⬜⬜⬜

☐ MasterCard ⬜⬜⬜⬜⬜⬜⬜⬜⬜⬜⬜⬜⬜⬜⬜⬜

Signature _____ Expiration Date _____

Name _____

Address _____

City _____ State _____ Zip _____

MAILING LABEL – PLEASE PRINT

FROM: Junior League of Colorado Springs, Inc.
P.O. Box 1058, Colorado Springs, CO 80901

TO: Name _____

Address _____

City _____

State _____ Zip _____